Accounting for Churches

Steven M. Bragg

AccountingTools®

ISBN-13: 978-1-64221-142-9

For more information about AccountingTools® products, visit our Web site at www.accountingtools.com.

Table of Contents

About the Author

Steven Bragg, CPA, has been the chief financial officer or controller of four companies, as well as a consulting manager at Ernst & Young. He received a master's degree in finance from Bentley College, an MBA from Babson College, and a Bachelor's degree in Economics from the University of Maine. He has been a two-time president of the Colorado Mountain Club, and is an avid alpine skier, mountain biker, and certified master diver. Mr. Bragg resides in Centennial, Colorado. He has written more than 300 books and courses, including *New Controller Guidebook*, *GAAP Guidebook*, and *Payroll Management*.

Steven maintains the accountingtools.com web site, which contains continuing professional education courses, the Accounting Best Practices podcast, and thousands of articles on accounting subjects.

Chapter 1
The Essentials of Church Accounting

Introduction

Some aspects of the accounting for churches are unique. They are not intended to earn a profit, they derive their income largely from donations, and direct their spending at such areas as worship, missions, and benevolent activities. Given these differences from what most non-religious organizations engage in, it should be no surprise that some of their accounting practices are different. In this chapter, we cover several concepts associated with nonprofit accounting, how the books of a church are set up, and what its financial statements look like.

The Nonprofit Aspects of Church Accounting

The primary difference between a church and a business organization is that a church is not concerned with making a profit, which means that it is classified as a nonprofit entity. This entity does not have owners, and has the purpose of serving society. The accounting standards relating to nonprofit entities are stated in Section 958 (Not-for-Profit Entities) of the Accounting Standards Codification, which is a consolidated version of Generally Accepted Accounting Principles (GAAP). GAAP is a cluster of accounting standards and common industry usage that has been developed over many years. It is used by organizations to do the following:

- Properly organize their financial information into accounting records;
- Summarize the accounting records into financial statements; and
- Disclose certain supporting information.

Under the United States tax laws, a nonprofit entity has tax-exempt status, so that it does not pay income taxes on that portion of its earnings that relate to its primary mission.

Fund Accounting

As just noted, churches operate as nonprofit entities. As such, they are required to use fund accounting. *Fund accounting* is a system for tracking the amount of cash assigned to different purposes and the usage of that cash. The intent of fund accounting is not to track whether a church has generated a profit, but rather how funds are used. It is also useful for tracking the amount of funds left for a specific activity; thus, if $20,000 is needed before a mission to Bolivia can be launched, then a shortfall of $2,000 from that amount is critical information for a church congregation to be aware of.

At the center of a system of fund accounting is the *fund*, which is a designated amount of resources that has been set aside for a specific purpose. Stated more simply, a fund is a major donation, where its use is tracked separately. For example, a congregation member contributes $50,000 to repave the church parking lot. This amount is recorded in a separate account, such as the "repaving project" account, so that all repaving expenditures can be subtracted from that account. The result is a centralized tracking system for cash inflows and outflows related to a specific purpose – repaving the parking lot.

We have just implied that a fund can be managed from a single account. This is possible, but a better approach is to have an accounting system that allows for an entirely separate general ledger for each fund. A *general ledger* is the master set of accounts that summarize all transactions occurring within a church – or, in this case, a fund that is part of the accounting records of a church. A fund's general ledger can then be used to aggregate information into a set of financial statements that report on that specific fund, showing the status for such activities as building maintenance, missions, and the purchase of a new church organ. Some of these financial reports may be quite simple, especially when the amounts involved are relatively small. For example, one might report that $22,000 was added to the Costa Rica mission fund in the last quarter, and then report outflows of $28,000 to support the mission, perhaps covering such expenses as travel, food, and building materials purchased for the construction of a school in Costa Rica. In other cases, such as for the construction of an entirely new church, the financial statements may need to be quite detailed, showing every aspect of the work that has been completed, and the expenditures made.

Funds are intended to restrict the uses to which certain cash flows can be put. For example, if a $10,000 donation is received for the purchase of a replacement church organ, then it is recorded within the organ fund, and so cannot be spent on any other activities, such as general facility maintenance. By taking this approach, a church has better control over its cash. Also, the operational results of a program can be compared to the expenditures coming from the fund that is supporting it, so that the church's vestry, council, or board (we will refer to it as the "board" through the remainder of this course) can evaluate the extent to which the program is meeting its goals.

A separate budget may be established for each fund. By doing so, the board can track the amount of expenditures against the level of available funding and manage the expenditure level so that the services provided via a fund are made available throughout the budget year without triggering a deficit in the amount of available funds.

Net Assets

An essential concept in church accounting is *net assets*, which is a church's total assets minus its total liabilities. Thus, net assets can be thought of as the residual amount owned by the church after all assets have been used to pay off all liabilities. This is the nonprofit version of the accounting equation, which is:

$$\text{Assets} = \text{Liabilities} + \text{Net Assets}$$

In a for-profit business, the formula uses equity instead of net assets, and is:

$$\text{Assets} = \text{Liabilities} + \text{Equity}$$

This relationship between assets, liabilities, and net assets can be seen in the statement of financial position (also known as the balance sheet), where the total of all assets always equals the sum of the liabilities and net assets sections.

When contributing assets, a donor may impose restrictions on their use. The result is two types of net assets, which are classified as net assets with donor restrictions and net assets without donor restrictions. The accounting for these types of net assets varies, as noted in the following sub-sections.

Net Assets without Donor Restrictions

When a donor imposes no restrictions on a contribution made to a nonprofit, the nonprofit records the contribution as an asset and as contribution revenue with no donor restrictions. Plate and pledge donations are usually classified as being unrestricted donations. These funds are used to pay for the general operations of a church. One should strongly encourage donors to make unrestricted donations, since these funds can be put to the broadest possible range of uses. Since this contribution revenue also creates a profit, the profit appears in the statement of financial position as an increase in net assets without donor restrictions.

Net Assets with Donor Restrictions

When a donor imposes a restriction on a contribution made to a church, the church records the contribution as contribution revenue with donor restrictions. Only the donor can change this designation; the board is not allowed to do so.

There may be a number of sub-accounts within the net assets with donor restrictions account, for those situations in which donors want to contribute to specific aspects of a project or to release funds for use over a period of time. For example, donors may only want to contribute to certain church activities – perhaps they feel strongly about supporting overseas missions, or maybe they just want to ensure that the church facility is properly maintained. Or, donors may want their contributions to be spent evenly over the next five years. It is also possible that donors will require that an asset be held by the church in perpetuity, usually allowing it to only spend any interest income derived from the funds.

Net Assets Summary

The following example shows various situations in which contributions fall into the two classifications.

EXAMPLE

Mr. Davis Templeton is a major contributor to the First Baptist Church. He is aware that the church needs $25,000 for an organ upgrade. He therefore contributes $25,000, under the provision that the funds will only be used for the upgrade. This contribution increases both the church's cash account and the net assets with donor restrictions account by $25,000. The church uses the money to complete the upgrade. The result is a shift of $25,000 from the cash account to the fixed assets account, as well as a shift of $25,000 from the net assets with donor restrictions account to the net assets without donor restrictions account.

EXAMPLE

Mrs. Martha Anglesey is a lifetime devotee of third-world schooling, and so contributes $500,000 to the First Baptist Church, under the provision that only the interest on the contribution can be spent, and only to pay for teachers in certain designated countries. This contribution increases the church's net assets with donor restrictions account by $500,000. In the first year of the endowment, $15,000 in interest is earned. The church records the $15,000 as a net asset with donor restrictions, until such time as the cash is paid out in teacher salaries.

The totals of each of these classifications are reported within the net assets section of the statement of financial position, along with a grand total for all net assets.

The Release from Restriction Concept

When funds are used in accordance with the wishes of a donor who had initially restricted the funds, they are considered to have been *released* from their initial restriction. This is a common event, and is reported within the revenue section of the statement of activities. In essence, funds released from restriction are stated as a fund reduction in the column for net assets with donor restrictions, and as a fund addition in the net assets without donor restrictions column. The net effect is zero. This concept appears in the case study at the end of this chapter. We show a portion of the statement of activities in that case study next, to show how $5,000 is released from the net assets with donor restrictions column and shifted to the net assets without donor restrictions column, with no effect on the church's revenues.

First Baptist Church
Statement of Activities
For the month ended February 28, 20X1

	Net Assets without Donor Restrictions	Net Assets with Donor Restrictions	Totals
Revenues:			
Contributions	$-	$-	$-
Net assets released from restrictions	5,000	-5,000	-
Total revenues	$5,000	-$5,000	$-

Cash vs. Accrual Basis Accounting

When recording revenues and expenses in its accounting records, a church can choose from either the cash basis or the accrual basis of accounting. Under the cash basis, revenue is recorded when cash is received, and expenses are recorded when cash is paid. Under the accrual basis, revenue is recorded when earned and expenses are recorded when consumed.

The main difference between the two methods is in the timing of transaction recordation. When aggregated over time, the results of the two methods are approximately the same. The timing difference between the two methods occurs because revenue recognition is delayed under the cash basis until donor payments arrive at the church. Similarly, the recognition of expenses under the cash basis can be delayed until such time as a supplier invoice is received. The following examples expand upon these concepts:

- *Revenue recognition.* A congregation member has been donating $1,000 each month to a church for years, under a written 20-year commitment. The March payment arrives a few days late, in early April. Under the cash basis, the church recognizes the donation in April, when the cash is received. Under the accrual basis, the church recognizes the donation in March, since the written commitment letter specifies monthly donations.
- *Expense recognition.* A church buys $500 of office supplies in May, which it pays for in June. Under the cash basis, the church recognizes the purchase in June, when it pays the bill. Under the accrual basis, the church recognizes the purchase in May, when it receives the supplier's invoice.

It is easiest to account for transactions using the cash basis, since no complex accounting transactions such as accruals are needed. Given its ease of use, the cash basis is widely used by churches. However, the relatively random timing of cash receipts and expenditures means that a church's reported financial results can vary widely from month to month.

Double Entry Accounting

Double entry accounting is a record keeping system under which every transaction is recorded in at least two accounts. There is no upper limit on the number of accounts used in a transaction, but the minimum is two accounts. There are two columns in each account, with debit entries on the left and credit entries on the right. In double entry accounting, the total of all debit entries must match the total of all credit entries. When this happens, a transaction is said to be *in balance*. If the totals do not agree, the transaction is *out of balance*. An out of balance transaction must be corrected before financial statements can be created.

The definitions of a debit and credit are:

- A debit is an accounting entry that either increases an asset or expense account, or decreases a liability or equity account. It is positioned to the left in an accounting entry.
- A credit is an accounting entry that either increases a liability or equity account, or decreases an asset or expense account. It is positioned to the right in an accounting entry.

An account is a separate, detailed record associated with a specific asset, liability, equity, revenue, expense, gain, or loss. Examples of accounts and their normal account balances appear in the following table.

Characteristics of Sample Accounts

Account Name	Account Type	Normal Account Balance
Cash	Asset	Debit
Pledges receivable	Asset	Debit
Fixed assets	Asset	Debit
Accounts payable	Liability	Credit
Mortgage	Liability	Credit
Unrestricted assets	Net Assets	Credit
Plate offerings	Revenue	Credit
Personnel – compensation	Expense	Debit
Property – facility maintenance	Expense	Debit
Administration – depreciation	Expense	Debit

The key point with double entry accounting is that a single transaction always triggers a recordation in *at least* two accounts, as assets and liabilities gradually flow through a church and are converted into revenues or expenses.

Journal Entries

A journal entry is a formalized method for recording an accounting transaction in a double entry accounting system, where the intent is to record every transaction in at least two places. For example, when a church receives a donation, this increases both the revenue account and the cash account. Or, if the church issues a paycheck to its minister, this increases both the compensation expense account and decreases the cash account.

The structure of a journal entry is:

- A header line may include a journal entry number and entry date.
- The first column includes the account number and account name into which the entry is recorded. This field is indented if it is for the account being credited.
- The second column contains the debit amount to be entered.
- The third column contains the credit amount to be entered.
- A footer line may also include a brief description of the reason for the entry.

Thus, the basic journal entry format is:

	Debit	Credit
Account name / number	$xx,xxx	
Account name / number		$xx,xxx

The structural rules of a journal entry are that there must be a minimum of two line items in the entry, and that the total amount entered in the debit column equals the total amount entered in the credit column.

Church Chart of Accounts

The chart of accounts is a list that states every account in the general ledger[1]. The chart usually begins with all asset accounts, followed by liability accounts, equity accounts, revenue accounts, and finally expense accounts. The following table contains a sample chart of accounts for a church, and includes an account number, account name, and account type. The accounts used in the table will not exactly match the needs of every church, but indicate the types of accounts that should be employed. Generally, the coding scheme aggregates accounts as follows:

1000-series numbers include all asset accounts
2000-series numbers include all liability accounts
3000-series numbers include all net asset accounts

---

[1] For a discussion of how the general ledger is used, see the author's *Bookkeeping Guidebook* course.

4000-series numbers include all revenue accounts
5000-series numbers include all operating expense accounts
6000-series numbers include all non-operating expense accounts

Sample Chart of Accounts

Account Number	Account Name	Account Type
1000	Cash – checking account	Asset
1010	Cash – savings account	Asset
1020	Investments	Asset
1200	Prepaid expenses	Asset
1300	Accounts receivable	Asset
1310	Pledges receivable	Asset
1500	Fixed assets – buildings	Asset
1510	Fixed assets – equipment	Asset
1520	Fixed assets – furniture and fixtures	Asset
1530	Fixed assets – land	Asset
1540	Fixed assets – vehicles	Asset
1550	Accumulated depreciation	Asset
2000	Accounts payable	Liability
2100	Payroll taxes	Liability
2200	Mission trip deposits	Liability
2300	Accrued liabilities	Liability
2400	Short-term notes payable	Liability
2500	Mortgages	Liability
2600	Long-term loans	Liability
3000	Unrestricted assets	Net Assets
3100	Restricted assets	Net Assets
4100	Operating income – plate offerings	Revenue
4110	Operating income – online giving	Revenue
4120	Operating income – pledges	Revenue
4130	Fund raiser income – parking lot	Revenue
4140	Fund raiser income – roof	Revenue
4150	Other income – bequests	Revenue
4160	Other income – weddings and funerals	Revenue
4170	Other income – bookstore	Revenue
5000	Cost of goods sold – bookstore	Expense

Account Number	Account Name	Account Type
5100	Personnel – compensation	Expense
5110	Personnel – benefits	Expense
5120	Personnel – housing	Expense
5130	Personnel – pension	Expense
5140	Personnel – training	Expense
5150	Property – facility maintenance	Expense
5160	Property – grounds maintenance	Expense
5170	Property – insurance	Expense
5180	Property – rent	Expense
5190	Property – utilities	Expense
5200	Programs – worship	Expense
5210	Programs – adult education	Expense
5220	Programs – youth education	Expense
5230	Programs – other	Expense
5240	Ministry – benevolence	Expense
5250	Ministry – community outreach	Expense
5260	Ministry – food pantry	Expense
5270	Administration – Internet	Expense
5280	Administration – office supplies	Expense
5290	Administration – dues and subscriptions	Expense
5300	Administration – postage	Expense
5310	Administration – professional services	Expense
5320	Administration – promotions	Expense
5330	Administration – telephones	Expense
5340	Administration – depreciation	Expense
6000	Interest expense	Expense
6100	Interest income	Expense

Bookkeeping Concerns

The bookkeeping for a church can be complicated, since donors may specify that their contributions only be used in certain ways. To make matters more complex, a donor may specify that certain proportions of their contributions be allocated to different types of expenditures. For example, a $10,000 donation may have attached to it a mandate that $1,000 can be spent on general church activities, while the remainder must be evenly split between two different funds. In this section, we note several options for reducing the burden on the bookkeeper when dealing with these difficult tracking chores. Possible options are:

- *Review reporting requirements in advance.* The reporting requirements imposed by some donors can be quite difficult to comply with, especially when a church's accounting systems are primitive. Accordingly, it can make sense to review a donor's reporting requirements prior to accepting any contributions. If the reporting is too difficult, negotiate hard for a simpler contribution restriction.
- *Use restricted sub-accounts.* Create a small number of sub-accounts within the general classification of net assets with donor restrictions and encourage donors to contribute into these prearranged sub-accounts. Doing so keeps a church from having to create a plethora of restricted accounts, each one dealing with the different restrictions imposed by each donor.

EXAMPLE

The Faith Baptist Church finds that its donors continually contribute funds under the provision that they be used only for specific missions. This has resulted in the use of more than 20 sub-accounts within the general classification of net assets with donor restrictions. To improve the situation, the board authorizes the creation of just three sub-accounts, which are for three specific missions. Donors are strongly encouraged to contribute to these sub-accounts, rather than targeting money at entirely new missions that may never be fully funded.

- *Flag negative balances.* The balance in any restricted net asset account should never drop below zero, since this implies that the church has spent more money than it has available. The accounting software should warn the bookkeeper when a transaction will drop one of these account balances below zero. If not, an ongoing staff activity should be to scan the account balances for negative amounts.
- *Document restrictions.* A church can get into trouble with its donors if it does not spend money in accordance with their wishes. To improve the odds of spending donated funds correctly, have each donor fill out a form on which is stated the name and address of the donor, the amount being contributed, and the nature of any restrictions. If the church has already set up restricted funds (such as for roof maintenance, building maintenance, or ministry outreach), then they can be conveniently stated on the form, with a checkoff box next to each one that donors can use to indicate their preferences. Then create a detailed listing of the restrictions placed on fund usage by donors, including the dates (if any) on which these restrictions are terminated. This document should be updated regularly, whenever funds with new restrictions are received, and when old restrictions are removed or the associated funds are spent.

Financial Statements

We have already referred to the financial statements that a church is expected to produce, and will return to the concept in the case study at the end of this chapter. For the moment, we will only describe the general structure of the two main financial statements used by a church, which are the statement of activities and the statement of financial position.

The statement of activities allows the board to view how much cash has been donated and how much of it has been used. An example statement appears in the following exhibit, where a variety of funds are stated across the top of the report, with their associated revenues and expenses broken out into separate columns. This layout gives an excellent view of the current status of all church operations.

First Congregational Church
Statement of Activities
for the Quarter Ended March 31, 20X2

	General Fund	Restricted Fund	Plant Fund	Endowment Fund	Total Funds
Revenue:					
Contributions	$290,000	$32,000	$19,000	$--	$341,000
Interest income	4,000	2,000	1,000	11,000	18,000
Workshop/events	6,000				6,000
Bequests				50,000	50,000
Total revenue	300,000	34,000	20,000	61,000	415,000
Expenses:					
Worship	100,000	7,000		13,000	120,000
Education	15,000	1,000			16,000
Care/fellowship	8,000				8,000
Evangelism	23,000				23,000
Resources	39,000				39,000
Community relief	5,000	2,000			7,000
Youth	4,000				4,000
Administration	110,000		10,000		120,000
Total expenses	304,000	10,000	10,000	13,000	337,000
Change in net assets	-$4,000	$24,000	$10,000	$48,000	$78,000
Beginning net assets	$62,000	$39,000	$443,000	$80,000	$624,000
Ending net assets	58,000	63,000	453,000	128,000	702,000

The statement of financial position is used to show the amount of assets, liabilities, and net assets on a church's books as of the date of the report. This report is quite useful for learning about such matters as the amount of cash currently on hand, the amount of receivables owed to the church, and the amounts it owes to others. It also breaks out unrestricted and restricted funds. An example statement appears in the following exhibit.

First Congregational Church
Statement of Financial Position
as of March 31, 20X2

	General Fund	Restricted Fund	Plant Fund	Endowment Fund	Total Funds
Assets:					
Cash	$59,000	$23,000	$19,000	$4,000	$105,000
Investments	15,000	40,000		124,000	179,000
Accounts receivable	2,000				2,000
Pledges receivable			14,000		14,000
Other current assets	6,000				6,000
Fixed assets			508,000		508,000
Total Assets	$82,000	$63,000	$541,000	$128,000	$814,000
Liabilities and Fund Balances:					
Accounts payable	$22,000			$3,000	$25,000
Payroll taxes	2,000				2,000
Short-term debt			8,000		8,000
Long-term debt			80,000		80,000
Total Liabilities	24,000	0	88,000	3,000	115,000
Fund Balances:					
Unrestricted	58,000	63,000			121,000
Restricted				125,000	125,000
Net investment in plant			453,000		453,000
Total Fund Balances	58,000	63,000	453,000	125,000	699,000
Total Liabilities and Fund Balances	$82,000	$63,000	$541,000	$128,000	$814,000

When the financial statements have been created for perusal by parties outside of the church, footnotes to the statements are usually included. In the following sample footnotes, we provide text that could be used to describe accounting policies and additional information that are specific to a church:

Cash Contributions

The Church recognizes cash contributions as revenue when they are received by the Church. Contributions received are recorded as being with or without restrictions, depending on whether any donor restrictions have been imposed. When a donor restriction expires (which occurs when a stipulated time restriction expires or a purpose restriction is accomplished), net assets with donor restrictions are reclassified to net assets without donor restrictions.

Investment Restrictions

Certain investments have been restricted because of agreements with donors, stipulating that the funds be held in perpetuity or are donor-restricted for the acquisition of fixed assets relating to Church property.

Net Assets

Net assets without donor restrictions are available for use by the Board for general operating and administrative purposes. The Board may designate a portion of these net assets for targeted purposes that makes them unavailable for use by management. In addition, the Board has designated a portion of these net assets for a contingency fund for facility upkeep. Net assets with donor restrictions are comprised of amounts limited by donor-imposed time or purpose restrictions.

Income Taxes

The Church is exempt from federal income taxation as an organization classified within Section 501(c)(3) of the Internal Revenue Code. In addition, the Church is classified as a public charity and not a private foundation for federal income taxation purposes. It has not incurred unrelated business income tax liabilities. Therefore, there is no income tax provision in the accompanying financial statements.

Net Assets with Donor Restrictions

Net assets with donor restrictions were constrained for the following purposes:

	Beginning Balance January 1	Contributions and Income	Releases	Ending Balance December 31
Building fund	$300,000	$120,000	-$170,000	$250,000
Endowments with distributions restricted for general ministry purposes	230,000	10,000	-15,000	225,000
Benevolence and other activities	20,000	75,000	-60,000	35,000
Missions	10,000	910,000	-890,000	30,000
Net appreciation on endowments	--	12,000	-8,000	4,000
Total	$560,000	$1,127,000	$1,143,000	$544,000

The Church has adopted an investment policy for endowment assets that is targeted at providing a consistent stream of funding to targeted programs, while preserving the invested capital. The Church relies upon the advice of investment counsellors, as well as its Board, when budgeting the amounts to be spent on supported programs. The Church has adopted an annual spending rate of 4% of the estimated fair value of the endowment funds.

Case Study

The use of journal entries and how they impact the financial statements of a church can be confusing, so we present in this section a case study that highlights the activities of the First Baptist Church to show what happens to the statement of activities and statement of financial position when each entry is made.

In the first transaction, a donor contributes $10,000 to assist in the startup of the church. The related journal entry is:

J/E #1	Debit	Credit
Cash [assets account]	10,000	
Donor contributions - unrestricted [revenue account]		10,000
To record receipt of donor contribution		

Since this is the first transaction that the church has ever had, the entry is the only one impacting the financial statements, which are as follows:

First Baptist Church
Statement of Financial Position
As of January 31, 20X1

ASSETS		LIABILITIES AND NET ASSETS	
Cash	$10,000	Accrued expenses	$-
Accounts receivable	-	Net assets:	
Fixed assets	-	Net assets without donor restrictions	10,000
Other assets	-	Net assets with donor restrictions	-
Total assets	$10,000	Total liabilities and net assets	$10,000

First Baptist Church
Statement of Activities
For the month ended January 31, 20X1

	Net Assets without Donor Restrictions	Net Assets with Donor Restrictions	Totals
Revenues:			
Contributions	$10,000	$-	$10,000
Net assets released from restrictions	-	-	-
Total revenues	$10,000	$-	$10,000
Expenses:			
Program expenses	$-		$-
Management and administration expenses	-		-
Total expenses	$-		$-
Change in net assets	$10,000	$-	$10,000
+ Beginning net assets	-	-	-
= Ending net assets	$10,000	$0	$10,000

In the second transaction, the church pays $1,000 to a landlord for office space. Of this amount, $400 is a deposit and $600 is the rent for the first month. The related journal entry is:

J/E #2	Debit	Credit
Deposits [assets account]	400	
Rent expense [expense account]	600	
Cash [asset account]		1,000
To record payment of monthly rent and a related security deposit		

This transaction reduces the cash balance, recognizes a $600 expense, and creates a deposit asset, as shown in the following financial statements. Also, note that these transactions are net of the previous $10,000 contribution that already appeared in the statements.

First Baptist Church
Statement of Financial Position
As of January 31, 20X1

ASSETS		LIABILITIES AND NET ASSETS	
Cash	$9,000	Accrued expenses	$-
Accounts receivable	-	Net assets:	
Fixed assets	-	Net assets without donor restrictions	9,400
Other assets	400	Net assets with donor restrictions	-
Total assets	$9,400	Total liabilities and net assets	$9,400

First Baptist Church
Statement of Activities
For the month ended January 31, 20X1

	Net Assets without Donor Restrictions	Net Assets with Donor Restrictions	Totals
Revenues:			
Contributions	$10,000	$-	$10,000
Net assets released from restrictions	-	-	-
Total revenues	$10,000	$-	$10,000
Expenses:			
Program expenses	$-		$-
Management and administration expenses	600		600
Total expenses	$-		$-
Change in net assets	$9,400	$-	$9,400
+ Beginning net assets	-	-	-
= Ending net assets	$9,400	$0	$9,400

In the third transaction, the donor contributes another $5,000, but this time mandates that the funds only be used to purchase a photocopier. This means that the funds are categorized as being restricted, as noted in the following journal entry.

J/E #3	Debit	Credit
Cash [assets account]	5,000	
Donor contributions – restricted [revenue account]		5,000
To record receipt of restricted donor contribution intended for photocopier purchase		

The impact on the January financial statements is that the funds are separately categorized from net assets without donor restrictions, as shown next.

First Baptist Church
Statement of Financial Position
As of January 31, 20X1

ASSETS		LIABILITIES AND NET ASSETS	
Cash	$14,000	Accrued expenses	$-
Accounts receivable	-	Net assets:	
Fixed assets	-	Net assets without donor restrictions	9,400
Other assets	400	Net assets with donor restrictions	5,000
Total assets	$14,400	Total liabilities and net assets	$14,400

First Baptist Church
Statement of Activities
For the month ended January 31, 20X1

	Net Assets without Donor Restrictions	Net Assets with Donor Restrictions	Totals
Revenues:			
Contributions	$10,000	$5,000	$15,000
Net assets released from restrictions	-	-	-
Total revenues	$10,000	$5,000	$15,000
Expenses:			
Program expenses	$-		$-
Management and administration expenses	600		600
Total expenses	$-		$-
Change in net assets	$9,400	$5,000	$14,400
+ Beginning net assets	-	-	-
= Ending net assets	$9,400	$5,000	$14,400

In the fourth transaction, the church uses the contributed $5,000 to purchase a photo-copier, and records the event with the following journal entry:

J/E #4	Debit	Credit
Fixed assets – equipment [assets account]	5,000	
Cash [assets account]		5,000
To record purchase of photocopier, using restricted funds		

This transaction shifts cash into a fixed asset, and also shifts the funds in net assets with donor restrictions to net assets without donor restrictions, as shown in the following financial statements. Note that the month in which the transaction occurs is February, which impacts the presentation in the statement of activities.

First Baptist Church
Statement of Financial Position
As of February 28, 20X1

ASSETS		LIABILITIES AND NET ASSETS	
Cash	$9,000	Accrued expenses	$-
Accounts receivable	-	Net assets:	
Fixed assets	5,000	Net assets without donor restrictions	14,400
Other assets	400	Net assets with donor restrictions	:
Total assets	$14,400	Total liabilities and net assets	$14,400

First Baptist Church
Statement of Activities
For the month ended February 28, 20X1

	Net Assets without Donor Restrictions	Net Assets with Donor Restrictions	Totals
Revenues:			
Contributions	$-	$-	$-
Net assets released from restrictions	5,000	-5,000	-
Total revenues	$5,000	-$5,000	$-
Expenses:			
Program expenses	$-		$-
Management and administration expenses	:		:
Total expenses	$-		$-
Change in net assets	$5,000	-$5,000	$-
+ Beginning net assets	9,400	5,000	14,400
= Ending net assets	$14,400	$-	$14,400

In all cases, note that the ending net asset total in the statement of financial position matches the ending net asset total in the statement of activities.

Summary

A church's bookkeeper must spend time creating the most appropriate recordkeeping structure when the system is first organized. This means deciding whether to use an accrual or cash basis system, developing an effective chart of accounts, and deciding how to account for each transaction type.

Nonprofit accounting is quite similar to project accounting, in that revenues and expenses are generally traceable to specific programs and operating activities. This is a more fine-grained level of detail than many for-profit organizations engage in, so more accounting effort is needed for a given level of activity in a church than in a for-profit business.

Chapter 2
Specific Accounting Transactions

Introduction

In this chapter, we will focus on a selection of the most critical accounting areas for a church, noting how the accounting should be handled. We pay particular attention to the accounting for offerings, payables, payroll, fixed assets, budgeting, and closing the books.

Accounting for Offerings

One of the main revenue sources for a church is the offering collected during church services. Key points related to the offering are as follows:

1. *Issue pre-stamped donation envelopes.* Issue to the congregation a number of donation envelopes that are pre-stamped with a few lines of text on the outside, on which someone can enter their name, contact information, and any intended purpose for the donated funds. This envelope is useful for hiding the amount of cash in the offering plate, and also for designating a targeted fund for each donation.
2. *Stamp "For Deposit Only."* All checks in the offering should be stamped in the endorsement block on the back with the words "For Deposit Only" followed by the church's bank account number, so that the checks cannot be fraudulently deposited elsewhere.
3. *Summarize the collection.* Once the collection has been completed, have two people jointly count the checks and cash in the plate and document this on the collection count sheet, a sample of which appears in the following exhibit. On the form, each check is listed separately, while all cash offerings are aggregated by bill type and coins. This is an essential control, since it is the focal point through which offerings are entered into a church's accounting system.

Sample Collection Count Sheet

Date:
_____

Check Amounts

1	$ _____	11	$ _____	21	$ _____
2	$ _____	12	$ _____	22	$ _____
3	$ _____	13	$ _____	23	$ _____
4	$ _____	14	$ _____	24	$ _____
5	$ _____	15	$ _____	25	$ _____
6	$ _____	16	$ _____	26	$ _____
7	$ _____	17	$ _____	27	$ _____
8	$ _____	18	$ _____	28	$ _____
9	$ _____	19	$ _____	29	$ _____
10	$ _____	20	$ _____	30	$ _____

Check Totals: _____

Cash Amounts

Number		Currency	Total
_____	×	$100	$ _____
_____	×	$50	$ _____
_____	×	$20	$ _____
_____	×	$10	$ _____
_____	×	$5	$ _____
_____	×	$1	$ _____
		Change	$ _____

Cash Totals: _____

Total Offering: _____

_____ _____ _____
Counter One Name   Counter One Signature   Date

_____ _____ _____
Counter Two Name   Counter Two Signature   Date

4. *Look for check errors.* Some checks may not be complete, so look for a missing payee name, a missing signature, or a difference between the numerical and written payment amount on the check. Any checks found with these problems will not be cashed by the bank, and so will need to be returned to the issuer for correction.

> **Note:** Encouraging congregation members to include their contact information on the offering envelope makes it easier to contact them if their check to the church is incomplete.

5. *Look for restrictions.* Review the memo section on each check to see if the donor has restricted the amount paid to a specific fund. If so, note the targeted funds on the collection count sheet.
6. *Record in the accounting system.* Record the summary totals from the collection count sheet in the accounting system, recording the transaction as of the date when the cash and checks were actually received.
7. *Record in donor records.* Record the amount received in the individual donor records, in order to maintain an ongoing tally of the amounts received, by donor.
8. *Create deposit slip.* Fill out a bank deposit slip and make a copy of it, to be retained in the accounting department.
9. *Transport to bank.* Transport the cash and checks to the bank as soon as possible, and obtain a deposit receipt from the bank teller. The amount stated on this receipt should match the amount stated on the deposit slip copy, indicating that nothing was stolen on the way to the bank.

Accounting for Payables

A church will typically receive a series of recurring invoices from a few suppliers that it uses on a regular basis. For example, it will probably use the same trash hauling service and the same florist for many years. In addition, invoices will sometimes arrive from other suppliers. The handling of these invoices is somewhat different, as we will see in the following process flow:

1. *Issue invoices for approval.* Send out all received invoices for approval. The approver should be the person responsible for the area to which the invoice pertains. Thus, the head of the facilities committee should approve a roofing repair invoice, while the pastor could approve the purchase of more general items, such as the monthly utilities bill.
2. *Match to receipts.* If an invoice was for a material item (as opposed to a service), match it to evidence that the item was received, to verify that the correct quantity was billed by the supplier.
3. *Load invoices into software.* When an invoice comes from a recurring source, access that supplier record in the accounting system and enter the invoice, noting whether the predetermined account code is correct for this invoice. If not, change the account code, so that the amount is charged to the correct

account. When the invoice comes from a new supplier, enter it as a one-time supplier; this means that the account code must be set up from scratch, so be extra careful about which one to use. For new suppliers, also ensure that the correct payment terms are loaded into the system, so that checks are not issued too soon.

4. *Print checks.* On a specific schedule, such as once a week, print all checks scheduled in the system for that week. Attach the supporting documentation to each check, and then bring the checks to the designated check signer to have them signed. It is best to remain there while the person signs the checks, in order to answer any questions that he or she may have.

5. *Disburse checks.* Separate check copies from the signed checks and mail the checks to suppliers. Then staple the check copies to the supporting documentation and file these packets by supplier name. If the payments were to one-time suppliers, then file them in a miscellaneous suppliers folder.

Note: If tracking expenditures by program, it may be necessary to split an invoice payment among several accounts – one for each program.

Accounting for Credit Card Payments

When a donor pays the church with a credit card, the credit card processing company removes a percentage of the payment as a fee. For example, a $100 donation might result in $96 appearing in the church's bank account. In this case, the journal entry to record the transaction requires that the processing fee be charged to a separate expense account. For example, the following journal entry shows the entry for a $100 donation:

	Debit	Credit
Cash [asset account]	96	
Bank fees [expense account]	4	
Operating income – online giving [revenue account]		100

Even though the church does not receive the full amount of the donor's original payment, the donor should always be credited with the full amount of the payment when issuing an acknowledgment letter.

Accounting for Reimbursements

Employees and congregation members routinely incur expenses on behalf of the church and want to be reimbursed. This is done using a standard form, on which they itemize the exact nature of each expenditure and the miles driven on behalf of the church. A sample format for such a form appears in the following exhibit.

Sample Expense Report Form

Employee Name		Expense Report Date						Expense Report		

Date	Expenditure Description	Airline	Rental Car	Meals	Tips	Supplies	Other	Totals
								+ Mileage Expense
								- Advances
								= Net Payable

Explanation of "Other" Items			Detail of Meals Expense			Detail of Mileage Expense			
Date	Description	Amount	Date	Description	Amount	Date	Description	Miles	$

Authorized By: [signature]		Date

Form 1099 Issuances

Following the end of the calendar year, a church needs to issue a Form 1099-NEC, *Nonemployee Compensation*, to any outside parties to which it paid compensation for services that exceeded $600 in the previous year. The form should be filed even when the payee was a corporation. The most likely situations in which this form must be filed by a church are when payments are made to accountants, architects, attorneys, contractors, engineers, or entertainers.

There are some exceptions that are not to be reported on the Form 1099-NEC. These are:

- Payments to corporations (except for those already noted)
- Payments for merchandise, telegrams, telephone, freight, storage, and similar items
- Payments of rent to real estate agents or property managers
- Wages paid to employees
- Business travel allowances paid to employees
- Payments to a tax-exempt organization
- Scholarship or fellowship grants

- Expense reimbursements paid to volunteers
- Payments for rent

Every Form 1099-NEC must also be furnished to the payment recipient.

Explanations of the key boxes on the form are noted in the following table. A sample Form 1099-NEC appears in the second exhibit.

Contents of Key 1099-NEC Fields

Box ID	Description
2nd TIN	2nd TIN notification – Check this box if you were notified by the IRS twice within the last three calendar years that the payee provided an incorrect taxpayer identification number. By marking this box, the IRS will send no further notices about this account.
Box 1	Nonemployee compensation – Includes all nonemployee compensation of $600 or more, subject to the limitations noted earlier in this section.
Box 4	Federal income tax withheld – Includes all backup withholding amounts. This typically involves individuals who have not furnished their taxpayer identification numbers to the church, which makes them subject to withholding.

Boxes 5-7 in the form are provided for the church's convenience and do not have to be filled out. They provide space for state-specific withholding and related information.

Sample Form 1099-NEC

The due date for filing a Form 1099-NEC is January 31 of the following calendar year.

Accounting for Payroll

There are a number of issues relating to the church accounting for payroll, ranging from the designation of a person as an employee to calculating payroll taxes and paying employees. We cover these topics and more in the following sub-sections.

Employee vs. Contractor Designation

When calculating payroll, a key determination for a church is whether someone can be classified as an employee or a contractor. This is a critical distinction, because an employee is paid through the payroll system, where the church is responsible for paying its portion of any payroll taxes, as well as for withholding any applicable income taxes from employee paychecks and remitting those taxes to the government. This is not the case for contractors.

The difference between an employee and a contractor centers on the relative independence of the positions. A contractor can create a deliverable for a church in any manner that he or she chooses. A person is an employee if the church controls not only the person's work output, but also the manner in which the work is performed. The IRS uses the following three criteria to establish whether someone is an employee:

- *Behavioral.* The church has the right to control how a person does his job.
- *Financial.* The church controls the business aspects of the person's job, such as providing compensation and reimbursement for expenses.
- *Relationship.* The church provides benefits to the person, or there is evidence of a similar situation that appears to indicate a long-term relationship.

There is no single test item that clearly shows a person to be an employee or a contractor. Rather, the decision is made based on the sum total of the preceding factors.

If a person is judged to be a contractor, then he or she is paid through the accounts payable system, rather than the payroll system. This means that the company is responsible for issuing a Form 1099 to the contractor shortly after the end of the calendar year, on which is stated the total amount paid to the contractor during the calendar year. The contractor (not the church) is responsible for paying all payroll taxes to the government.

EXAMPLE

A bookkeeper comes in once a week to process transactions for a church, run checks, and issue financial statements. The church is one of her 12 clients. The bookkeeper is likely to be classified as a contractor. However, if the church board mandates that she work a specified number of hours per week and gives her specific procedures to follow in performing the work, she is more likely to be classified as an employee.

EXAMPLE

A local man mows the church lawn once every other week for a fixed fee, and does so on his own schedule. He is classified as a contractor.

EXAMPLE

The church secretary works at the church for 20 hours per week, is paid a fixed sum per hour, and is subject to the direction of the minister. She is classified as an employee.

A minister is generally classified as an employee, since he or she works under the direction of a board, which also pays for the minister's office space and reimburses all business expenses. However, a supply pastor may be classified as a contractor, since this individual serves on a limited basis as the acting pastor.

Definition of a Minister

Ministers receive special treatment under the Internal Revenue Code, so it is important to understand how the IRS defines a minister. Here is the IRS definition:

> Most services you perform as a minister, priest, rabbi, etc., are ministerial services. These services include:
>
> - Performing sacerdotal functions;
> - Conducting religious worship; and
> - Controlling, conducting, and maintaining religious organizations (including the religious boards, societies, and other integral agencies of such organizations) that are under the authority of a religious body that is a church or denomination.
>
> You are considered to control, conduct, and maintain a religious organization if you direct, manage, or promote the organization's activities.
>
> A religious organization is under the authority of a religious body that is a church or denomination if it is organized for and dedicated to carrying out the principles of a faith according to the requirements governing the creation of institutions of the faith.

It can be useful to clarify which positions are not considered to be minister positions for tax purposes. They include non-ordained persons, deacons, and youth ministers.

Payroll Tax Rules Pertaining to Churches

The following rules apply to payroll taxes and income tax withholding for churches that are exempt from paying the federal income tax under section 501(c)(3) of the Internal Revenue Code:

- *Federal income tax.* The church must withhold federal income taxes from employee pay in the normal manner.
- *Social security and Medicare taxes.* The church must deduct the normal amount of these taxes, unless the organization pays an employee less than $100 per calendar year or it is a church opposed to the payment of these taxes for religious reasons that has filed Form 8274, *Certification by Churches and Qualified Church-Controlled Organizations Electing Exemption from*

Employer Social Security and Medicare Taxes. In the latter case, employees must pay the self-employment tax instead.

- *Federal unemployment tax.* The church is exempt from this tax, which also means that the organization does not have to file Form 940, *Employer's Annual Federal Unemployment Tax Return.*

- *Ministers – taxes.* The earnings of a minister are not subject to federal income tax withholding, nor are social security and Medicare deductions made by the church. Instead, the minister must pay the full 15.3% self-employment tax, as well as federal income tax, as though he or she were self-employed (which is not the case if the minister is a member of a religious order whose members have taken a vow of poverty). Though the church is not responsible for these items, it can reach an agreement with the minister to voluntarily withhold taxes to cover the minister's liability for the self-employment tax and federal income tax.

- *Ministers – compensation.* A minister should include in his or her gross income any fees received for the performance of wedding, funerals, and so forth, as well as gifts from the congregation.

- *Ministers – housing.* When ministers are given a housing allowance or live in a church-provided parsonage, this benefit is exempt from income taxation, but is subject to social security and Medicare taxation. We expand upon this topic in the next sub-section.

Tax Treatment of Minister Housing

A minister who performs ministerial services as an employee may be able to exclude from gross income the fair rental value of a home provided as part of compensation (a parsonage) or a housing allowance provided as compensation if it is used to rent or otherwise provide a home. A minister who is furnished a parsonage may exclude from gross income the fair rental value of the parsonage, including utilities. However, the amount excluded cannot be more than reasonable compensation for the minister's services.

> **Tip:** If there is a real estate agent in the congregation, consult with this person regarding what the fair rental value of the parsonage may be, and document it in case the IRS conducts an audit.

A minister who receives a housing allowance may exclude the allowance from gross income to the extent that it is used to pay expenses in providing a home. Generally, those expenses include rent, mortgage interest, utilities, and other expenses directly related to providing a home[2]. The amount excluded cannot be more than reasonable compensation for the minister's services.

---

[2] Other expenses related to providing a home include home improvements, minor repairs, home décor, lawn care, cable television, and Internet service.

EXAMPLE

Minister Alfred Dunn rents a home. His rental payments total $18,000 per year, his utilities are $4,000 per year, and his home maintenance costs $3,000 per year, which total $25,000 per year. His church is paying him $45,000 per year and his housing allowance is $28,000 annually. He can exclude the $25,000 of actual expenses from his gross income, though he must report the $3,000 excess housing allowance as income. The amount excluded from gross income is well below his $45,000 compensation, so it does not run afoul of the IRS regulations in this regard.

If a minister owns his own home, he may still claim deductions for mortgage interest and real property taxes. If his housing allowance exceeds the lesser of his reasonable compensation, the fair rental value of the home, or the actual expenses directly related to providing the home, then the amount of the excess income must be included.

In order to be able to exclude the housing allowance from income, the church must officially designate the housing allowance as such before paying it to the minister.

> **Tip:** Have the board formally state the amount of the housing allowance in its minutes, and renew this statement at the start of each year – thereby clearly documenting the nature and amount of the allowance.

The fair rental value of a parsonage or the housing allowance is excludable only for income tax purposes. The minister must include the amount of the fair rental value of a parsonage or the housing allowance for social security coverage purposes.

EXAMPLE

David Smithers is the minister of the Faith Baptist Church. His base compensation is $48,000 per year, and the fair rental value of his parsonage is $20,000 per year. In addition, utilities cost $3,000 per year. Therefore, his income for the calculation of self-employment income taxes is $71,000.

The Payroll Cycle

One of the more important payroll management decisions is how long to set the payroll cycle. Each payroll requires a great deal of effort to collect information about time worked, locate and correct errors, process wage rate and deduction changes, calculate pay, and issue payments. Consequently, it makes sense to extend the duration of payroll cycles.

If payrolls are spaced at short intervals, such as weekly, then paychecks must be prepared 52 times per year. Conversely, paying employees once a month reduces the payroll preparation activities by approximately three-quarters. Since paying employees just once a month can be a burden on the employees, one might consider a half-way measure, which is paying employees either twice a month (the *semimonthly* payroll) or once every two weeks (the *biweekly* payroll). The semimonthly payroll cycle results in processing 24 payrolls per year, while the biweekly payroll cycle requires the processing of 26 payrolls per year.

An argument in favor of the biweekly payroll is that employees become accustomed to receiving two paychecks per month, plus two "free" paychecks during the year, which has a somewhat more positive impact on employee morale. Nonetheless, the semimonthly payroll represents a slight improvement over the biweekly payroll from the perspective of bookkeeping efficiency, and is therefore recommended.

Employment Eligibility Verification

Before hiring an employee, a church must verify that the person is eligible to work. This is done by filling out the Form I-9, which requires it to attest to the immigration status of its employees. In the form, the prospective employee presents appropriate types of identification, and the employer verifies these documents. There are several allowable forms of evidence; in essence, a person can present a single document that proves both identity and employment authorization (such as a U.S. passport or a permanent resident card) or two documents, one proving identity (such as a driver's license) and the other proving employment authorization (such as a social security card).

Withholdings Documentation

One of the inputs used to calculate payroll is the Form W-4, which is needed to calculate the amount of federal income tax to withhold from employee pay. An example of a completed Form W-4 is shown on the following two pages. Every employee should complete a Form W-4 when hired, but they are not required by law to do so. If a Form W-4 is not received from an employee, then the church withholds income taxes as though the person were single, with no adjustments (which results in the maximum possible income tax withholding).

Form W-4, Employee's Withholding Certificate (page 1)

Form **W-4**	**Employee's Withholding Certificate**	OMB No. 1545-0074
Department of the Treasury Internal Revenue Service	Complete Form W-4 so that your employer can withhold the correct federal income tax from your pay. **Give Form W-4 to your employer.** Your withholding is subject to review by the IRS.	2024

Step 1: Enter Personal Information	**(a)** First name and middle initial John D.	Last name Smith	**(b)** Social security number 012-34-5678
	Address 420 Evangelical Way		**Does your name match the name on your social security card?** If not, to ensure you get credit for your earnings, contact SSA at 800-772-1213 or go to *www.ssa.gov.*
	City or town, state, and ZIP code Bethesda, MD 20810		

(c) ☐ Single or Married filing separately

☑ Married filing jointly or Qualifying surviving spouse

☐ Head of household (Check only if you're unmarried and pay more than half the costs of keeping up a home for yourself and a qualifying individual.)

Complete Steps 2–4 ONLY if they apply to you; otherwise, skip to Step 5. See page 2 for more information on each step, who can claim exemption from withholding, and when to use the estimator at *www.irs.gov/W4App.*

Step 2: **Multiple Jobs or Spouse Works**	Complete this step if you (1) hold more than one job at a time, or (2) are married filing jointly and your spouse also works. The correct amount of withholding depends on income earned from all of these jobs. Do **only one** of the following. **(a)** Use the estimator at *www.irs.gov/W4App* for most accurate withholding for this step (and Steps 3–4). If you or your spouse have self-employment income, use this option; **or** **(b)** Use the Multiple Jobs Worksheet on page 3 and enter the result in Step 4(c) below; **or** **(c)** If there are only two jobs total, you may check this box. Do the same on Form W-4 for the other job. This option is generally more accurate than (b) if pay at the lower paying job is more than half of the pay at the higher paying job. Otherwise, (b) is more accurate . . . . ☐

Complete Steps 3–4(b) on Form W-4 for only ONE of these jobs. Leave those steps blank for the other jobs. (Your withholding will be most accurate if you complete Steps 3–4(b) on the Form W-4 for the highest paying job.)

Step 3: Claim Dependent and Other Credits	If your total income will be $200,000 or less ($400,000 or less if married filing jointly): Multiply the number of qualifying children under age 17 by $2,000 $ 2000 Multiply the number of other dependents by $500 . . . . . $ Add the amounts above for qualifying children and other dependents. You may add to this the amount of any other credits. Enter the total here	**3**	$ 2000

Step 4 **(optional):** Other Adjustments	**(a) Other income (not from jobs).** If you want tax withheld for other income you expect this year that won't have withholding, enter the amount of other income here. This may include interest, dividends, and retirement income	**4(a)**	$
	(b) Deductions. If you expect to claim deductions other than the standard deduction and want to reduce your withholding, use the Deductions Worksheet on page 3 and enter the result here	**4(b)**	$
	(c) Extra withholding. Enter any additional tax you want withheld each **pay period** . .	**4(c)**	$ 100

Step 5: Sign Here	Under penalties of perjury, I declare that this certificate, to the best of my knowledge and belief, is true, correct, and complete.
	_____ **Employee's signature** (This form is not valid unless you sign it.) **Date**

Employers Only	Employer's name and address St. Bartholomew Church 300 Pastoral Lane Bethesda, MD 20810	First date of employment 2/1/24	Employer identification number (EIN) 84-1234567

For Privacy Act and Paperwork Reduction Act Notice, see page 3.   Cat. No. 10220Q   Form **W-4** (2024)

Form W-4, Employee's Withholding Certificate (page 2)

Step 2(b) — Multiple Jobs Worksheet *(Keep for your records.)*

If you choose the option in Step 2(b) on Form W-4, complete this worksheet (which calculates the total extra tax for all jobs) on **only ONE** Form W-4. Withholding will be most accurate if you complete the worksheet and enter the result on the Form W-4 for the highest paying job. To be accurate, submit a new Form W-4 for all other jobs if you have not updated your withholding since 2019.

Note: If more than one job has annual wages of more than $120,000 or there are more than three jobs, see Pub. 505 for additional tables; or, you can use the online withholding estimator at *www.irs.gov/W4App*.

1. **Two jobs.** If you have two jobs or you're married filing jointly and you and your spouse each have one job, find the amount from the appropriate table on page 4. Using the "Higher Paying Job" row and the "Lower Paying Job" column, find the value at the intersection of the two household salaries and enter that value on line 1. Then, **skip** to line 3 . . . . **1** $ _____

2. **Three jobs.** If you and/or your spouse have three jobs at the same time, complete lines 2a, 2b, and 2c below. Otherwise, skip to line 3.

   a. Find the amount from the appropriate table on page 4 using the annual wages from the highest paying job in the "Higher Paying Job" row and the annual wages for your next highest paying job in the "Lower Paying Job" column. Find the value at the intersection of the two household salaries and enter that value on line 2a . . . . **2a** $ _____

   b. Add the annual wages of the two highest paying jobs from line 2a together and use the total as the wages in the "Higher Paying Job" row and use the annual wages for your third job in the "Lower Paying Job" column to find the amount from the appropriate table on page 4 and enter this amount on line 2b . . . . **2b** $ _____

   c. Add the amounts from lines 2a and 2b and enter the result on line 2c . . . . **2c** $ _____

3. Enter the number of pay periods per year for the highest paying job. For example, if that job pays weekly, enter 52; if it pays every other week, enter 26; if it pays monthly, enter 12, etc. . . . . . . **3** _____

4. **Divide** the annual amount on line 1 or line 2c by the number of pay periods on line 3. Enter this amount here and in **Step 4(c)** of Form W-4 for the highest paying job (along with any other additional amount you want withheld) . . . . **4** $ _____

Step 4(b) — Deductions Worksheet *(Keep for your records.)*

---

1. Enter an estimate of your 2024 itemized deductions (from Schedule A (Form 1040)). Such deductions may include qualifying home mortgage interest, charitable contributions, state and local taxes (up to $10,000), and medical expenses in excess of 7.5% of your income . . . . **1** $ _____

2. Enter: { • $29,200 if you're married filing jointly or a qualifying surviving spouse
   • $21,900 if you're head of household
   • $14,600 if you're single or married filing separately } . . . . . **2** $ _____

3. If line 1 is greater than line 2, subtract line 2 from line 1 and enter the result here. If line 2 is greater than line 1, enter "-0-" . . . . **3** $ _____

4. Enter an estimate of your student loan interest, deductible IRA contributions, and certain other adjustments (from Part II of Schedule 1 (Form 1040)). See Pub. 505 for more information . . . . **4** $ _____

5. **Add** lines 3 and 4. Enter the result here and in **Step 4(b)** of Form W-4 . . . . **5** $ _____

Gross Pay Calculations

The simplest and most commonly-used method for determining the compensation of an hourly employee is the hourly rate plan, under which hours worked are multiplied by an employee's hourly rate. This method can be more complicated if there is a shift differential or overtime. A shift differential is extra pay earned by employees who work a less than desirable shift, such as the evening, night, or weekend shifts.

EXAMPLE

Arlo Montaigne works the night shift as a janitor at the First Christian Church. He earns a base wage of $13.50 per hour, plus a $0.50 shift differential. In the most recent work week, he logs 39 hours of work. The calculation of his wages earned under the hourly rate plan is:

($13.50 base wage + $0.50 shift differential) × 39 hours = $546.00

If there is a shift differential, add it to the base wage prior to calculating overtime.

What if an employee works a fraction of an hour? A computerized payroll system automatically converts this to a fraction of an hour. However, a bookkeeper that manually calculates wages may use a variety of simplification methods, such as rounding up to the nearest quarter-hour.

EXAMPLE

Grace Baptist Church's bookkeeper calculates wages for its employees by hand. In the most recent week, Mortimer Davis worked 39 hours and 41 minutes. The bookkeeper could use a calculator to determine that 41 minutes is 0.6833 hours (calculated as 41 minutes ÷ 60 minutes) and pay the employee on that basis. However, prior calculation errors have led to a policy of rounding up to the next quarter hour. Accordingly, the bookkeeper rounds the 41 minutes up to 45 minutes, and therefore records 39 ¾ hours for Mr. Davis.

Payroll Tax Calculations

The next step is to withhold taxes from employee pay. First of all, what are these taxes? They include the following:

- *Social security tax.* This is used to fund a national pension plan for workers. The tax rate is 6.2% on the first $168,600 of an employee's wages (as of 2024). The amount is matched by the employer.
- *Medicare tax.* This is used to fund a medical care plan that is mostly available to those over 65 years old. The tax rate is 1.45% and there is no cap on the compensation amount to which it applies. The amount is matched by the employer.

> **Note:** Churches are exempt from federal unemployment taxes, though they may need to pay state-level unemployment taxes, depending on the state.

The IRS provides a set of wage bracket tables for income tax withholdings in its Publication 15-T, *Federal Income Tax Withholding Methods*. This publication is available as a PDF download on the www.irs.gov website. The IRS recommends that, if an employer is computing its payroll manually, it should use the following worksheet as the basis for determining federal income taxes payable for each employee.

Worksheet 2. Employer's Withholding Worksheet for Wage Bracket Method Tables for Manual Payroll Systems With Forms W-4 From 2020 or Later

Keep for Your Records

Table 4	Monthly	Semimonthly	Biweekly	Weekly	Daily
	12	24	26	52	260

Step 1. Adjust the employee's wage amount

1a Enter the employee's total taxable wages this payroll period .... 1a $ _____

1b Enter the number of pay periods you have per year (see Table 4) .... 1b _____

1c Enter the amount from Step 4(a) of the employee's Form W-4 .... 1c $ _____

1d Divide the amount on line 1c by the number of pay periods on line 1b .... 1d $ _____

1e Add lines 1a and 1d .... 1e $ _____

1f Enter the amount from Step 4(b) of the employee's Form W-4 .... 1f $ _____

1g Divide the amount on line 1f by the number of pay periods on line 1b .... 1g $ _____

1h Subtract line 1g from line 1e. If zero or less, enter -0-. This is the **Adjusted Wage Amount** ...... 1h $ _____

Step 2. Figure the Tentative Withholding Amount

2a Use the amount on line 1h to look up the tentative amount to withhold in the appropriate Wage Bracket Table in this section for your pay frequency, given the employee's filing status and whether the employee has checked the box in Step 2 of Form W-4. This is the **Tentative Withholding Amount** .... 2a $ _____

Step 3. Account for tax credits

3a Enter the amount from Step 3 of the employee's Form W-4 .... 3a $ _____

3b Divide the amount on line 3a by the number of pay periods on line 1b .... 3b $ _____

3c Subtract line 3b from line 2a. If zero or less, enter -0- .... 3c $ _____

Step 4. Figure the final amount to withhold

4a Enter the additional amount to withhold from Step 4(c) of the employee's Form W-4 .... 4a $ _____

4b Add lines 3c and 4a. **This is the amount to withhold from the employee's wages this pay period** .... 4b $ _____

The wage bracket tables are designed to be an easy way to derive the correct amount of income tax withholding for people at lower wage levels (up to $100,000 per year). Each table calculates the proper amount of withholding under a different set of scenarios. An extract from a wage bracket table is shown in the following exhibit, which is taken from a recent version of Publication 15-T. The table lists the amount of income tax withholding for someone being paid on a weekly basis, and states the proper withholding for three types of taxpayer – married filing jointly, head of household, and single or married filing separately. The actual full-length table presents information for a much larger range of income.

2024 Wage Bracket Method Tables for Manual Payroll Systems with Forms W-4 From 2020 or Later
WEEKLY Payroll Period

If the Adjusted Wage Amount (line 1h) is		Married Filing Jointly		Head of Household		Single or Married Filing Separately	
At least	But less than	Standard withholding	Form W-4, Step 2, Checkbox withholding	Standard withholding	Form W-4, Step 2, Checkbox withholding	Standard withholding	Form W-4, Step 2, Checkbox withholding
		The Tentative Withholding Amount is:					
$775	$785	$22	$55	$37	$65	$55	$93
$785	$795	$23	$57	$38	$66	$57	$95
$795	$805	$24	$58	$39	$68	$58	$98
$805	$815	$25	$59	$40	$69	$59	$100
$815	$825	$26	$60	$41	$70	$60	$102
$825	$835	$27	$61	$43	$72	$61	$104
$835	$845	$28	$63	$44	$75	$63	$106
$845	$855	$29	$64	$45	$77	$64	$109
$855	$865	$30	$65	$46	$79	$65	$111
$865	$875	$31	$66	$47	$81	$66	$113
$875	$885	$32	$67	$49	$83	$67	$115
$885	$895	$33	$69	$50	$86	$69	$117
$895	$905	$34	$70	$51	$88	$70	$120
$905	$915	$35	$71	$52	$90	$71	$122
$915	$925	$36	$72	$53	$92	$72	$124
$925	$935	$37	$73	$55	$94	$73	$126
$935	$945	$38	$75	$56	$97	$75	$128
$945	$955	$39	$76	$57	$99	$76	$131
$955	$965	$40	$77	$58	$101	$77	$133
$965	$975	$41	$78	$59	$103	$78	$135
$975	$985	$42	$79	$61	$105	$79	$137
$985	$995	$43	$81	$62	$108	$81	$139
$995	$1,005	$44	$82	$63	$110	$82	$142
$1,005	$1,015	$45	$83	$64	$112	$83	$144
$1,015	$1,025	$46	$84	$65	$114	$84	$146

To use the wage bracket method, go to the table that corresponds to the church's payroll. Within that table, go to the adjusted wage amount that applies to the employee in question, and then go across the table to find the correct taxpayer type for that employee. The amount in this cell is the amount of income tax to withhold.

EXAMPLE

Albert Montaigne works for the Trinity Lutheran Church. Mr. Montaigne is an hourly employee of the church, which pays its staff on a weekly basis. Mr. Montaigne earned $780 during the most recent weekly period. He stated on his Form W-4 that he is filing as a head of household. According to the preceding extract from the IRS wage bracket table, the church should deduct a total of $37 from his wages to cover his income tax withholdings.

Benefits and Other Deductions

Thus far, we have described a set of mandatory deductions from gross pay related to taxes. In addition, there are a number of other deductions that may be taken from gross pay. The essential information related to these deductions is described in the following bullet points:

- *Benefits deductions*. A church that wants to retain its employees over the long term may offer them a benefits package that could include medical, dental, vision, life, short-term and long-term disability insurance. The amount deducted from employee pay is typically the residual amount owed after the church pays for a portion of the underlying expense.
- *Charitable contributions*. Many employers encourage their employees to make contributions to local or national charities, and may also match these

contributions to some extent. Under such an arrangement, an employee signs a pledge card, which authorizes the employer to deduct certain contribution amounts from their pay on an ongoing basis. The employer then periodically forwards the sum total of all contributions deducted to the targeted charities, along with any matching amount that the employer is paying.

- *Garnishments.* Some people resist fulfilling their legal obligations to other parties, or they do not have the financial resources to do so. If a church employs such a person, it is quite possible that the bookkeeper will receive a garnishment order, under which the church must withhold specified amounts from an employee's pay and forward it to a third party. A garnishment order usually relates to child support, unpaid taxes, or unpaid student loans.
- *Deductions for financing repayments.* A church may issue advances or loans to its employees. If so, deductions from future paychecks will be needed to reduce the balances of these outstanding amounts.

Net Pay

Net pay is the amount paid to employees after the deductions described in the previous sections are deducted from gross pay. The entire net pay calculation may be included in a remittance advice that is forwarded to employees along with their paychecks. A typical calculation format that may be given to an employee is as follows:

Gross pay (40 hours × $30.00/hour)	$1,200.00
Deductions:	
Social security	74.40
Medicare	17.40
Income tax withholding	225.00
Medical insurance	160.00
Garnishments	115.00
Net pay	$608.20

Payroll Tax Remittances

A church has a legal obligation to forward to the government all income taxes that it has withheld from employee pay, as well as social security and Medicare taxes. These remittances must be forwarded to the government in accordance with a specific payment schedule and method that is described in the following sub-sections. In this section, we review when tax deposits should be made, how to remit funds, and related reporting requirements.

If a church were to miss a timely remittance, or pay an insufficient amount, the related penalty would be severe. For this reason alone, it is important to have a detailed understanding of tax remittances.

Types of Tax Deposit Schedules

There are two deposit schedules, known as the monthly deposit schedule and the semiweekly deposit schedule that state when to deposit payroll taxes. The bookkeeper must determine which of these deposit schedules will be followed before the beginning of each calendar year. The selection of a deposit schedule is based entirely on the tax liability reported during a lookback period.

The deposit schedule is based on the total taxes (i.e., federal income taxes withheld, social security taxes, and Medicare taxes) reported in line 8 of the Forms 941 in a four-quarter lookback period. The lookback period begins on July 1 and ends on June 30. The decision tree for selecting a deposit period is:

- If the church reported $50,000 or less of taxes during the lookback period, use the monthly deposit schedule.
- If the church reported more than $50,000 of taxes during the lookback period, use the semiweekly deposit schedule.

EXAMPLE

The Calvary Baptist Church had used the monthly deposit schedule in previous years, but its payroll expanded considerably in the past year, which may place it in the semiweekly deposit schedule. The bookkeeper calculates the amount of taxes paid during its lookback period to see if the semiweekly deposit schedule now applies. The calculation is:

Lookback Period	Taxes Paid
July 1 – September 30, 2023	$8,250
October 1 – December 31, 2023	14,750
January 1 – March 31, 2024	17,500
April 1 – June 30, 2024	19,000
Total	$59,500

Since the total amount of taxes that the church paid during the lookback period exceeded $50,000, it must use the semiweekly deposit schedule during the next calendar year.

The schedule for depositing state withholding taxes varies by state. Consult with the applicable state government for this deposit schedule. If the church outsources payroll processing, the supplier will handle these deposits on the church's behalf.

Monthly Deposit Schedule

If a church qualifies to use the monthly deposit schedule (which is usually the case), deposit employment taxes on payments made during a month by the 15th day of the following month.

EXAMPLE

The New Hope Baptist Church is a monthly schedule depositor that pays its staff on the 15th and last business day of each month. Under the monthly deposit schedule, New Hope must deposit the combined tax liabilities for all of its payrolls in a month by the 15th day of the following month. The same deposit schedule would apply if New Hope had instead paid its employees every day, every other week, twice a month, once a month, or on any other payroll schedule.

The total payroll taxes withheld for each of New Hope's payrolls in September are noted in the following table, along with the amount of its tax liability that will be due for remittance to the government on October 15:

	Federal Income Tax Withheld	Social Security Tax Withheld	Medicare Tax Withheld
Sept. 15 payroll	$1,500.00	$620.00	$145.00
Sept. 30 payroll	1,250.00	558.00	130.50
Sept. total withheld	$2,750.00	$1,178.00	$275.50
Employer tax matching	--	1,178.00	275.50
Tax deposit due Oct. 15	$2,750.00	$2,356.00	$551.00

New Hope's tax liability to be remitted on October 15 is $5,657.00, which is calculated as the total of all withholdings and employer matches for federal income taxes, social security taxes, and Medicare taxes ($2,750.00 + $2,356.00 + $551.00).

Semiweekly Deposit Schedule

If a church qualifies to use the semiweekly deposit schedule, remit payroll taxes using the following exhibit.

Semiweekly Deposit Schedule

Payment Date	Corresponding Deposit Date
Wednesday, Thursday, or Friday	Following Wednesday
Saturday, Sunday, Monday, Tuesday	Following Friday

If a church has more than one pay date during a semiweekly period and the pay dates fall in different calendar quarters, make separate deposits for the liabilities associated with each pay date.

EXAMPLE

The First Presbyterian Church has a pay date on Wednesday, June 29 (second quarter) and another pay date on Friday, July 1 (third quarter). It must make a separate deposit for the taxes associated with each pay date, even though both dates fall within the same semiweekly period. The church should pay both deposits on the following Wednesday, July 6.

EXAMPLE

The Seventh-Day Adventist Church uses the semiweekly deposit schedule. It only pays its employees once a month, on the last day of the month. Although it is on a semiweekly deposit schedule, it can only make a deposit once a month, since it only pays its employees once a month.

Note that the semiweekly deposit method does not mean that a church is required to make two tax deposits per week – it is simply the name of the method. Thus, if a church has one payroll every other week, it would remit taxes only every other week.

The differentiating factor between the monthly and semiweekly deposit schedules is that a church must remit taxes much more quickly under the semiweekly method. The monthly method uses a simpler and more delayed tax deposit schedule, which is ideal for smaller churches.

Remittance Method

All federal tax deposits must be paid by electronic funds transfer. Use the Electronic Federal Tax Payment System (EFTPS) to make these deposits. EFTPS is a free service that is maintained by the Department of Treasury. The system can either be used directly or through an intermediary, such as a church's payroll supplier (if the business is outsourcing payroll) to deposit the funds on the church's behalf. Go to www.eftps.gov to enroll in EFTPS. If the church is a new employer, it will likely have been pre-enrolled in EFTPS when it applied for an employer identification number (EIN); if so, it will receive a personal identification number for the EFTPS system as part of the initial EIN package of information.

When remitting taxes to the government, the remittance should include the following types of taxes:

- Withheld income taxes
- Withheld and matching employer social security taxes
- Withheld and matching employer Medicare taxes

When a deposit is made, EFTPS will provide a deposit trace number, which can be used as a receipt or to trace the payment.

Payroll Journal Entries

The primary journal entry for payroll includes debits for wages and the employer's portion of payroll taxes. There will also be credits to a number of other accounts, each one detailing the liability for payroll taxes that have not been paid, as well as for the amount of cash already paid to employees for their net pay. The basic entry is:

	Debit	Credit
Wages expense [expense account]	xxx	
Payroll taxes expense [expense account]	xxx	
Cash [asset account]		xxx
Federal withholding taxes payable [liability account]		xxx
Social security taxes payable [liability account]		xxx
Medicare taxes payable [liability account]		xxx
Garnishments payable [liability account]		xxx

Note: The reason for the payroll taxes expense line item in this journal entry is that the employer incurs the cost of matching the social security and Medicare amounts paid by employees. The employee-paid portions of the social security and Medicare taxes are not recorded as expenses; instead, they are liabilities for which the church has an obligation to remit cash to the taxing government entity.

A key point with this journal entry is that the wages expense contains employee gross pay, while the amount actually paid to employees through the cash account is their net pay. The difference between the two figures (which can be substantial) is the amount of deductions from their pay, such as payroll taxes and withholdings to pay for benefits.

There may be a number of additional employee deductions to include in this journal entry. For example, there may be deductions for pension plans, health insurance, life insurance, vision insurance, and for the repayment of advances.

When the church later pays the withheld taxes and its portion of payroll taxes, use the following entry to reduce the balance in the cash account and eliminate the balances in the liability accounts:

	Debit	Credit
Federal withholding taxes payable [liability account]	xxx	
Social security taxes payable [liability account]	xxx	
Medicare taxes payable [liability account]	xxx	
State withholding taxes payable [liability account]	xxx	
Garnishments payable [liability account]	xxx	
Cash [asset account]		xxx

Thus, when a church initially deducts taxes and other items from an employee's pay, the church incurs a liability to pay the taxes to a third party. This liability only disappears from the church's accounting records when it pays the related funds to the party to which they are owed.

Payroll Tax Returns

Following each calendar quarter, any church that pays wages subject to income tax withholding, or social security and Medicare taxes, must file a Form 941, the Employer's Quarterly Federal Tax Return. The Form 941 must be filed by the last day of the month following the calendar quarter to which it applies. It is used to reconcile the monthly payments made to the total liability for the quarter, and also notes the total number of employees, and the totals for wages paid and withholdings.

Following the end of every calendar year, and no later than January 31, a church must issue the multi-part Form W-2, on which it itemizes the wages it paid to each employee during the year, as well as the taxes that it withheld from employee pay. It issues this form to anyone who was paid wages by the church at any time during the year, even if they no longer work for it. This information forms the basis for the personal income tax returns completed by all employees for the federal government and the state government in which they reside. An example of the Form W-2 is shown next.

Sample Form W-2

The Form W-2 contains a large number of fields, but many of them are not needed to report the compensation and tax information for a typical church employee; many of the fields are only required to report unusual compensation arrangements. The payroll system prints these forms automatically after the end of the calendar year. If the church is outsourcing payroll, the supplier will issue them on its behalf. Thus, the Form W-2 is usually not an especially difficult document to produce.

Accounting for Fixed Assets

Fixed assets are property that is intended to be used for an extended period of time, such as a church building, the church organ, and any vehicles owned by the church. There are several key points in the life of a fixed asset that require recognition in the accounting records; these are the initial recordation of the asset, the recognition of depreciation, and the eventual derecognition of the asset. There may also be cases in which the value of an asset is impaired. We describe these general concepts in the following bullet points and again later in the following sub-sections:

- *Initial recognition*. There are a number of factors to consider when initially recording a fixed asset, such as the base unit, which costs to include, and when to stop capitalizing costs.
- *Depreciation*. The cost of a fixed asset is gradually charged to expense over time, using depreciation.
- *Impairment*. There are numerous circumstances under which an asset's recorded value is considered to be impaired. If so, the value of the asset is written down on the books of the church.
- *Derecognition*. When an asset comes to the end of its useful life, the church will likely sell or otherwise dispose of it. At this time, remove it from the accounting records, as well as record a gain or loss (if any) on the final disposal transaction.

The Capitalization Limit

One of the most important decisions to be made in the initial recognition of a fixed asset is what minimum cost level to use, below which an expenditure is recorded as an expense in the period incurred, rather than as a fixed asset. This capitalization limit, which is frequently abbreviated as the *cap limit*, is usually driven by the following factors:

- *Asset tracking*. If an expenditure is recorded as a fixed asset, the fixed asset tracking system may impose a significant amount of control over the newly-recorded fixed asset. This can be good, if the bookkeeper needs to know where an asset is at any time.
- *Fixed asset volume*. The number of expenditures that will be recorded as fixed assets will increase dramatically as the cap limit is lowered. For example, there may only be one fixed asset if the cap limit is $100,000, 50 assets if the cap limit is $10,000, and 500 assets if the cap limit is $1,000. Analyze historical expenditures to estimate a cap limit that will prevent the bookkeeper from being deluged with additional fixed asset records.

- *Record keeping*. The bookkeeper can spend an excessive amount of time tracking fixed assets, formulating depreciation and eliminating fixed assets from the records once they have been disposed of. This can be quite a burden if there are many assets.

From an efficiency perspective, a high cap limit is always best, since it greatly reduces the work of the bookkeeper. From an asset tracking perspective, the reverse situation is the most favorable, with a very low cap limit. These conflicting objectives call for some discussion within the board about the most appropriate cap limit – it should not simply be imposed on the church by the bookkeeper.

The Base Unit

There is no specific guidance in the accounting standards about the unit of measure for a fixed asset. This unit of measure, or *base unit*, is essentially a church's definition of what constitutes a fixed asset. This definition can be formalized into a policy, so that it is applied consistently over time. Here are several issues to consider when creating a definition of a base unit:

- *Aggregation*. Should individually insignificant items be aggregated into a fixed asset, such as a group of tables or chairs? This increases the administrative burden, but does delay recognition of the expense associated with the items.
- *Component replacement*. Is it likely that large components of an asset will be replaced during its useful life? If so, designate the smaller units as the most appropriate base unit to track in the accounting records. This decision may be influenced by the probability of these smaller components actually being replaced over time. For example, the roof of a church could be designated as a separate asset, since it may be replaced several times over the life of the building.
- *Identification*. Can an asset that has been designated as a base unit be physically identified? If not, it will be impossible to track the asset, so it should not be designated as a base unit. This is a common problem in a church that may have dozens of identical tables, chairs, and other furniture.
- *Useful life*. The useful lives of the components of a base unit should be similar, so that the entire unit can be eliminated or replaced at approximately the same time.

The Initial Measurement of a Fixed Asset

Initially record a fixed asset at the historical cost of acquiring it, which includes the costs to bring it to the condition and location necessary for its intended use. These activities include the following:

- Physical construction of the asset
- Demolition of any preexisting structures
- Renovating a preexisting structure to alter it for use by the buyer

- Administrative and technical activities during preconstruction, such as designing the asset and obtaining permits
- Administrative and technical work after construction commences, such as litigation, labor disputes, and technical problems

---

EXAMPLE

The board of the Zion Lutheran Church decides to add an additional air conditioning unit to its main administration building, which involves the creation of a concrete pad for the unit, stringing electrical cabling to it, linking it to the building's air conditioning vents, and obtaining an electrical permit. All of the following costs can be included in the fixed asset cost of the unit:

Air conditioning unit price	$50,000
Concrete pad	3,000
Wiring and ducts	5,000
Electrical permit	200
Total	$58,200

A church may receive donations of fixed assets. These donations are recorded at their fair value as of the date of donation. This recorded fair value then becomes the cost basis for the asset. Donated assets are depreciated in the normal manner, as described in the following sections.

The Purpose of Depreciation

The purpose of depreciation is to charge to expense a portion of an asset that relates to the revenue generated by that asset. This is called the matching principle, where revenues and expenses both appear in the statement of activities in the same reporting period, which gives the best view of how well a church has performed in a given period. The trouble with this matching concept is that there is usually only a tenuous connection between the generation of revenue and a specific asset.

To get around this linkage problem, we usually assume a steady rate of depreciation over the useful life of each asset, so that we approximate a linkage between the recognition of revenues and expenses. If we were not to use depreciation at all, we would be forced to charge all assets to expense as soon as we buy them. This would result in large losses in the months when this purchase transaction occurs, followed by unusually high profitability in those periods when the corresponding amount of revenue is recognized, with no offsetting expense. Thus, a church that does not use depreciation will have front-loaded expenses and extremely variable financial results.

Depreciation Concepts

There are three factors to consider in the calculation of depreciation, which are as follows:

- *Useful life.* This is the time period over which it is expected that an asset will be productive, or the amount of activity expected to be generated by it. Past its useful life, it is no longer cost-effective to continue operating the asset, so the church would dispose of it or stop using it. Depreciation is recognized over the useful life of an asset.

> **Tip:** Rather than recording a different useful life for every asset, it is easier to assign each asset to an asset class, where every asset in that asset class has the same useful life. This approach may not work for very high-cost assets, where a greater degree of precision may be needed.

- *Salvage value.* When a church eventually disposes of an asset, it may be able to sell the asset for some reduced amount, which is the salvage value. Depreciation is calculated based on the asset cost, less any estimated salvage value. If salvage value is expected to be quite small, it is generally ignored for the purpose of calculating depreciation.

EXAMPLE

Calvary Baptist Church buys a van for $40,000 and estimates that its salvage value will be $10,000 in five years, when it plans to dispose of the asset. This means that the church will depreciate $30,000 of the asset cost over five years, leaving $10,000 of the cost remaining at the end of that time. The church's bookkeeper expects to then sell the asset for $10,000, which will eliminate it from the accounting records.

- *Depreciation method.* Depreciation expense can be calculated using an accelerated depreciation method, or evenly over the useful life of the asset. Churches typical employ a steady depreciation rate, since it is easy to calculate. The primary method for steady depreciation is the straight-line method, which is discussed next.

Straight-Line Method

The straight-line method depreciates an asset at the same standard rate throughout its useful life. The straight-line calculation steps are:

1. Subtract the estimated salvage value of the asset from the amount at which it is recorded on the books.
2. Determine the estimated useful life of the asset. It is easiest to use a standard useful life for each class of assets.

3. Divide the estimated useful life (in years) into 1 to arrive at the straight-line depreciation rate.
4. Multiply the depreciation rate by the asset cost (less salvage value).

EXAMPLE

The United Methodist Church buys a copier machine for $6,000. It has an estimated salvage value of $1,000 and a useful life of five years. The church's bookkeeper calculates the annual straight-line depreciation for the copier as:

1. Purchase cost of $6,000 – Estimated salvage value of $1,000 = Depreciable asset cost of $5,000

2. 1 ÷ 5-Year useful life = 20% Depreciation rate per year

3. 20% Depreciation rate × $5,000 Depreciable asset cost = $1,000 Annual depreciation

---

The Depreciation of Land

Nearly all fixed assets have a useful life, after which they no longer contribute to the operations of a church or they stop generating revenue. During this useful life, they are depreciated, which reduces their cost to what they are supposed to be worth at the end of their useful lives. Land, however, has no definitive useful life, so there is no way to depreciate it.

The Depreciation of Land Improvements

Land improvements are enhancements to a plot of land to make it more usable. If these improvements have a useful life, depreciate them. If there is no way to estimate a useful life, do not depreciate the cost of the improvements.

If land is being prepared for its intended purpose, include these costs in the cost of the land asset. They are not depreciated. Examples of such costs are:

- Demolishing an existing building
- Clearing and leveling the land

If functionality is being added to the land and the expenditures have a useful life, record them in a separate Land Improvements account. Examples of land improvements are:

- Drainage and irrigation systems
- Fencing
- Landscaping
- Parking lots and walkways

A special item is the ongoing cost of landscaping. This is a period cost, not a fixed asset, and so should be charged to expense as incurred.

EXAMPLE

The First Baptist Church buys a parcel of land for $1,000,000. Since it is a purchase of land, the church cannot depreciate the cost. It then razes a building that was located on the property at a cost of $25,000, fills in the old foundation for $5,000 and levels the land for $50,000. All of these costs are to prepare the land for its intended purpose, so they are all added to the cost of the land. The church cannot depreciate these costs.

The intent is to use the land as a parking lot for church facilities, so $350,000 is spent to create a parking lot. The church's bookkeeper estimates that these improvements have a useful life of 10 years. She should record this cost in the Land Improvements account and depreciate it over 10 years.

Depreciation Accounting Entries

The basic depreciation entry is to debit the depreciation expense account (which appears in the statement of activities) and credit the accumulated depreciation account (which appears in the statement of financial position as a contra account that reduces the amount of fixed assets). Over time, the accumulated depreciation balance will continue to increase as more depreciation is added to it, until such time as it equals the original cost of the asset. At that time, stop recording any depreciation expense, since the cost of the asset has now been reduced to zero.

The journal entry for depreciation can be a simple two-line entry designed to accommodate all types of fixed assets, or it may be subdivided into separate entries for each type of fixed asset.

EXAMPLE

The bookkeeper for the First Baptist Church calculates that it should have $7,000 of depreciation expense in the current month. The entry is:

	Debit	Credit
Depreciation expense	7,000	
Accumulated depreciation		7,000

In the following month, the bookkeeper decides to show a higher level of precision at the expense account level, and instead elects to apportion the $7,000 of depreciation among different expense accounts, so that each class of asset has a separate depreciation charge. The entry is:

	Debit	Credit
Depreciation expense – buildings	4,000	
Depreciation expense – equipment	1,500	
Depreciation expense – furniture and fixtures	1,000	
Depreciation expense – vehicles	500	
Accumulated depreciation		7,000

Accumulated Depreciation

When an asset is sold or otherwise disposed of, remove all related accumulated depreciation from the accounting records at the same time. Otherwise, an unusually large amount of accumulated depreciation will build up on the statement of financial position.

EXAMPLE

The Grace Baptist Church has $1,000,000 of fixed assets, for which it has charged $380,000 of accumulated depreciation. This results in the following presentation in its statement of financial position:

Fixed assets	$1,000,000
Less: Accumulated depreciation	(380,000)
Net fixed assets	$620,000

The church then sells an organ for $80,000 that had an original cost of $140,000, and for which it had already recorded accumulated depreciation of $50,000. It records the sale with this journal entry:

	Debit	Credit
Cash	80,000	
Accumulated depreciation	50,000	
Loss on asset sale	10,000	
Fixed assets		140,000

As a result of this entry, the church's statement of financial position presentation of fixed assets has changed, so that fixed assets before accumulated depreciation have declined to $860,000 and accumulated depreciation has declined to $330,000. The new presentation is:

Fixed assets	$860,000
Less: Accumulated depreciation	(330,000)
Net fixed assets	$530,000

The amount of net fixed assets declined by $90,000 as a result of the asset sale, which is the sum of the $80,000 cash proceeds and the $10,000 loss resulting from the asset sale.

Asset Disposal Accounting

There are two scenarios under which a business may dispose of a fixed asset. The first situation arises when a fixed asset is being eliminated without receiving any payment in return. This is a common situation when a fixed asset is being scrapped because it is obsolete or no longer in use and there is no resale market for it. In this case, reverse any accumulated depreciation and reverse the original asset cost. If the asset is fully depreciated, that is the extent of the entry.

EXAMPLE

A church buys a used copier for $10,000 and recognizes $1,000 of depreciation per year over the following ten years. At that time, the copier is not only fully depreciated, but also ready for the scrap heap. The church gives away the copier for free and records the following entry.

	Debit	Credit
Accumulated depreciation	10,000	
Equipment asset		10,000

A variation on this situation is to write off a fixed asset that has not yet been completely depreciated. In this case, write off the remaining undepreciated amount of the asset to a loss account.

EXAMPLE

To use the same example, the church gives away the copier after eight years, when it has not yet depreciated $2,000 of the asset's original $10,000 cost. In this case, it records the following entry:

	Debit	Credit
Loss on asset disposal	2,000	
Accumulated depreciation	8,000	
Equipment asset		10,000

Another scenario arises when an asset is sold, so that the church receives cash in exchange for the fixed asset being sold. Depending upon the price paid and the remaining amount of depreciation that has not yet been charged to expense, this can result in either a gain or a loss on sale of the asset.

EXAMPLE

The church still disposes of its $10,000 used copier, but does so after seven years and sells it for $3,500 in cash. In this case, it has already recorded $7,000 of depreciation expense. The entry is:

	Debit	Credit
Cash	3,500	
Accumulated depreciation	7,000	
Gain on asset disposal		500
Equipment asset		10,000

What if the church had sold the copier for $2,500 instead of $3,500? Then there would be a loss of $500 on the sale. The entry would be:

	Debit	Credit
Cash	2,500	
Accumulated depreciation	7,000	
Loss on asset disposal	500	
Equipment asset		10,000

The "loss on asset disposal" or "gain on asset disposal" accounts noted in the preceding sample entries are called *disposal accounts*. They may be combined into a single account or used separately to store gains and losses resulting from the disposal of fixed assets.

Budgeting Best Practices

The concept of developing a detailed budget is well beyond the scope of this course, since it can involve quite detailed compilations of projected revenues and expenditures (see the author's *Budgeting* course for a comprehensive discussion of budget models). Instead, we will focus on a number of best practices to consider when formulating a budget, so that a model can be developed that most closely adheres to the desires of the church board. Our essential points are as follows:

- *Build the budget in layers.* Start with the core functions of the church, without including any programs that are not essential to its ongoing survival. Make sure that there are sufficient revenues coming from donations to pay for these core functions before layering on any non-essential programs. For example, strip out all missionary support in the first draft of the budget, and just see if current donation levels will pay for the minister and basic facility support functions.

- *Examine donations by probability tranches.* Donations probably follow the 80/20 rule, where 80% of the donations come from 20% of the congregation. When this is the case, review in detail the 20% paying most of the donations, and estimate how likely it is that they will continue to do so. Some of them will likely retire and so will have reduced incomes from which to make donations – so if replacements cannot be identified, it may be necessary to budget for reduced revenues in the upcoming year.

EXAMPLE

Mrs. Griffin has reliably donated $3,000 per year to the church in each of the past 10 years. However, she recently told the minister that she is moving 500 miles to be closer to her daughter and grandson. It would be reasonable to assume that her donations to the church will end as soon as she moves.

> **Tip:** Ask congregation members for their pledge commitments for the upcoming year. Doing so may unearth donation problems, so that the budget can be adjusted before the new year begins.

- *Adjust for economic conditions.* Adjust the projected donation figures from the preceding step for expected changes in economic conditions. These estimates tend to be highly localized, such as evaluating rumors of the closure of a nearby production facility where many members of the congregation work. This review can give the board an early warning sign that there may be donation problems looming.

- *Identify program funding.* Identify the exact sources of funding for specific programs, and *then* budget the associated expenses. It is quite possible that some funding sources will no longer be available, in which case the congregation will need to find alternative revenue sources, or decide to drop some programs entirely. A minimum amount of revenue is usually needed to fund a program, so if this threshold cannot be attained, then the decision should be made to drop the affected program. Otherwise, the board will spend hours trying to shift over funds from alternative sources to fund a program that is not viable.

- *Identify bequests*. When a bequest is received from a member of the congregation, budget for how it will be used based on the certain knowledge that this money will eventually run out. This means specifically linking certain expenditures in the budget to a bequest, so that everyone knows this is a one-time event. For example, when a bequest is used to pay for a new parking lot, identify the source of the money, so that no one is operating under the false assumption that this money will be available again in the following year for more capital expenditures.

- *Estimate normal cost increases*. Some costs are going to increase, such as pay raises for the minister and other staff, utilities, and so forth. Include these estimates in the budget as early as possible, since they are needed to determine the increased amount of revenue that the church needs in order to break even.

- *Examine projected maintenance expenditures*. Churches require more maintenance as they age, so take a hard look at anything that can break during the upcoming year, and budget an appropriate amount for it. Alternatively, if the decision is made to defer maintenance, then develop a schedule of when it is supposed to be paid for, in order to have a rational discussion about just how long some actions can be deferred.

- *Examine program needs*. Review every projected expenditure for every program, to see if it is adequate for the associated program goals. If not, estimate what the expenditures actually need to be, or whether the goals should be scaled back. Also, discuss the probability of continuing to receive the supporting grants that were used to fund these programs in the past.

- *Look for step costs*. Evaluate whether there are any step costs (which tend to increase sharply at discrete points). For example, the addition of an assistant minister who is intended to take on additional church services represents a major step cost, since this person's compensation presumably also includes benefits and housing. This investigation is particularly important for programs, where someone may need to be hired to oversee each one.

- *Identify breakeven point*. Compile a list of every fixed cost, such as minister compensation, utilities, and building maintenance. Then take a hard look at the historical variability of donations to offset these fixed costs, and evaluate whether there is likely to be sufficient cash to break even during the year.

- *Estimate ongoing cash levels*. For each month in the budget, estimate the amount of cash that will be on hand after all bills have been paid. This gives the board advance warning of any projected cash shortfalls, so that they can begin to plan for it, such as by delaying expenditures until after a lean month has passed. This is a particular concern when the church has minimal cash reserves.

EXAMPLE

Members of the Church of the Nazarene are most generous with their donations at Christmas and Easter, when the church collects 20% of its total annual donations. Conversely, its average donation rate typically declines by 30% during the summer months, when members of the congregation are away on their summer vacations. When this seasonality is factored into the annual budget, the board finds that there will be an $8,000 cash shortfall at the end of July.

- *Fund future asset purchases*. The church will occasionally need to replace existing assets, such as the church van – or perhaps it will need a new copier in a few years. Rather than waiting until the year in which these expenditures must be made, budget for a set-aside in each year leading up to the purchase, so that the money will be available when needed.
- *Earn a surplus*. Spending every penny that a church earns is not a good way to run it, since doing so leaves no fund for a rainy day. Instead, make an attempt in the budget to earn a surplus – however small it may be – in order to give the church a buffer for those years in which unexpected expenditures arise.
- *Load the budget into the accounting software*. Once the budget is complete and has been approved by the board, load it into the accounting software, so that it can be used to construct budget versus actual reports. These reports are useful for spotlighting unexpected revenue declines or expense spikes.
- *Review quarterly*. Actual revenue and expense results will inevitably diverge from expectations. Perhaps a key donor died, or the church organ required an unexpected repair. To adjust for these issues, review the budget each quarter and revise it as needed. Doing so this frequently gives the board time to cut spending when revenues are trending too low, thereby cutting losses before they can accumulate.

Many of the preceding best practices had a conservative slant. While it would be wonderful for a church to gain a sudden boost of unexpected wealth, the more common situation is for it to have a quite steady stream of revenue that cannot be expected to increase forever. This means that budgets are likely to be tight, especially when the congregation is not increasing in size.

Closing Best Practices

The monthly financial statements need to be as accurate as possible, so that the board is not blindsided by unusually high or low results. We have itemized the following best practices to assist in generating the most accurate church financial statements:

- *Record online donations*. If the church accepts online donations, verify that they have been properly recorded in the accounting system.
- *Log investment income*. Record the amount of investment income associated with the church's investments during the month.

- *Wait for invoices*. It can make sense to wait a day or two after month-end to see if any additional supplier invoices arrive in the mail. Also, issue a notice to the staff to submit their expense reports. The intent is to ensure that all expenses have been collected.
- *Log interest expense*. If the church has any loans outstanding, determine the amount of this expense during the month and record it in the accounting system.
- *Account for cash*. Verify that all cash receipts have been recorded in the accounting system, and that these items have then been deposited at the bank.
- *Assign charges*. Ensure that all credit card charges have been assigned to the appropriate programs. It can help to send a preliminary version of each program's financial results to the responsible party, with a note to review the document and report back if any revenue or expense items do not look accurate.
- *Pay payroll taxes*. Verify that all payroll taxes were remitted to the government in a timely manner. This means reviewing the remittance documentation, as well as the contents of the payroll liabilities account for evidence of payment.
- *Charge off prepaid expenses*. If any expenditures were initially recorded in the prepaid expenses asset account, review it each month to verify that a monthly charge was made to reflect periodic usage of these expenditures.
- *Load in bank statement items*. Access the monthly bank statement and use it to load interest income and bank fees into the accounting system. This may also include automatic withdrawals from the account.
- *Conduct bank reconciliation*. Reconcile the monthly bank statement to the church's cash account, making any adjustments as needed. This will likely result in a list of deposits in transit, as well as a list of outstanding checks.
- *Reconcile accounts*. Examine the contents of every asset and liability account to verify that its contents are valid. In particular, this step keeps items from building up in asset accounts when they should have been charged off earlier in the year. At a minimum, the contents of the accounts receivable, pledges receivable, and accounts payable accounts should always be matched to the supporting detail, to ensure that they are accurate. A large amount of transaction volume flows through these accounts, so it is more likely that the supporting detail will differ from their associated account balances.
- *Examine preliminary financials*. It is quite possible that some transactions were recorded in the wrong account, so review a preliminary copy of the financial statements to see if this is the case. This task is made easier if the budget was already recorded in the accounting system, so that actual results can be compared to the budget. Another approach is to load the financial statements into a multi-month spreadsheet, so that results can be examined on a multi-month trend line – this approach is useful for spotting anomalies or trends.

An additional task for the end of the year is to print a year-end book. This book includes the year-end financial statements and trial balance, which constitute the results for the entire year. The book should also include the general ledger, as well as the detail for the ending asset and liability balances; this means adding the accounts receivable aging report, accounts payable aging report, and fixed assets register to the book. All of these supporting documents should have totals that exactly match what is in the general ledger. Why compile this information? Because it constitutes a printed record of all church business transactions during the year. As such, it can be quite valuable for auditors, and especially if its electronic records are destroyed.

Document Retention

The bookkeeper should archive church accounting records for the period of time indicated in the following table. The active period stated in the schedule shows the amount of time that records should be retained on the premises, while the inactive period shows the additional time during which records should be retained in archival storage.

Records Retention Schedule

Record Types	Active Period (Years)	Inactive Period (Years)	Total Period (Years)
Accounting and Finance			
Bank statements	2	3	5
Financial statements	3	7	10
General ledger	3	7	10
Payables ledger	2	8	10
Receivables ledger	2	8	10
Organization			
Annual audit reports	Permanent	--	Permanent
Board minutes	Permanent	--	Permanent
Capitalization schedule	Permanent	--	Permanent
Bylaws	Permanent	--	Permanent
Property deeds	Permanent	--	Permanent
Property insurance policies	Permanent	--	Permanent
Administration			
Contracts	5	5	10
Contribution records	2	5	7
Donor credit card numbers	0	0	0
Gift restriction records	7 years after funds expended	--	7 years after funds expended

A variety of legislation has mandated the minimum periods over which human resources records must be maintained. The following table states these intervals, and the minimum employer size for which the storage requirement is mandated.

Human Resources Records Retention Schedule

Record Type	Retention Period	Minimum Employer Size
Benefit payments	3 years	20+ employees
COBRA notice issuances	6 years	20+ employees
COBRA procedures	6 years	20+ employees
Compensation records	3 years	20+ employees
Deductions from pay	2 years	No minimum
Disability status	1-2 years	Depends on size
Employee benefit plans	1 year after plan termination	20+ employees
Employment applications	1 year	15+ employees
Employment contracts	3 years	No minimum
Employment test results	1 year	20+ employees
FMLA* disputes documentation	3 years	50+ employees
FMLA* leave dates	3 years	50+ employees
FMLA* notices	3 years	50+ employees
FMLA* premium payments for benefits	3 years	50+ employees
I-9 Form	Later of 3 years or 1 year after employment	4+ employees
Income tax withholding documentation	4 years	No minimum
Injury logs	5 years	11+ employees
Job announcements	1 year	No minimum
Minority and female applicant records	3 years	No minimum
Personal information (name, address, social security number, gender, date of birth, occupation, and job classification)	3 years	20+ employees
Pre-employment records for temporary positions	1 year	20+ employees
Promotions and demotions	1 year	15+ employees
Reasonable accommodation requests	1 year	15+ employees
Records of hours worked	3 years	20+ employees
Records related to discrimination charges	Until resolved	15+ employees
Resumes	1 year	15+ employees
Salary calculations	3 years	No minimum

Record Type	Retention Period	Minimum Employer Size
Tax deductions	3 years	20+ employees
Terminations	1 year	15+ employees
Training records	1 year	20+ employees
Training records for safety and health topics	3 years	11+ employees
Veteran status	1-2 years	Depends on size
Work schedules	2 years	No minimum

* Family and Medical Leave Act

State and local laws may mandate longer retention intervals, so periodically check local regulations to see if they override the intervals noted here. Also, these retention periods are only the minimums. It may make sense to retain records for longer periods of time to ensure that the church has an adequate defense in case a lawsuit is filed prior to the expiration of any applicable statute of limitations.

Accounting Policies

A church needs just a few accounting policies to give some structure to how it handles certain types of transactions. These policies should be approved by the board, and reviewed periodically to see if they still meet the needs of the church. We recommend the following policies:

- *Acceptance of cash donor-restricted gifts.* The board must approve cash donor-restricted gifts that are not targeted at existing funds. This policy is needed to ensure that these gifts align with the church's mission.
- *Acceptance of noncash property.* The board must approve all prospective gifts of noncash property. Some of these donations can require out-of-pocket costs for the church, so the board needs to decide whether it is financially cost-effective to accept them.
- *Release of donor-restricted funds.* Only a member of the board is authorized to release funds that have been restricted by a donor. This could be done at the beginning of the year for blocks of planned expenditures, rather than requiring specific approval for each disbursement.
- *Reimbursements.* The church will only reimburse for expenses incurred solely for the benefit of the church, and for which receipts have been provided within 60 days of the event. The board must pre-approve any expenditures on behalf of the church that exceed $___. Valid expenses that will be reimbursed include mileage at the current federal rate for charitable organizations, parking, tolls, travel expenses, office supplies and furnishings, books, and postage.
- *Items not reimbursed.* The church will not reimburse for any of the items noted in the following table.

List of Non-Reimbursement Items

Adult entertainment	Expenses > 90 days old	Personal reading material
Car washes and cleaning	Finance charges on credit cards	Theft/loss of personal property
Contributions	Health club / spa fees	Toiletries
Child care	Laundry fees on short-duration trips	Traffic fines
Clothing	Lost luggage	Travel insurance
Commuting costs	Movies	Undocumented expenses

Summary

The general types of accounting transactions that a church will encounter match those of any other nonprofit entity. However, there are some areas in which the bookkeeper should pay particular attention. One is certainly the handling of cash and checks from members of the congregation, since there is a high risk of errors and theft here. Another is the accounting for reimbursements, since both staff and volunteers may make expenditures on behalf of the church, and want to be paid back. This calls for the use of a standard reimbursement procedure that is closely adhered to in order to ensure that reimbursements are accurate. Yet another area of concern is whether someone is an employee or contractor for payroll purposes. A church may find that several parties are in a gray area, where they could be treated either way. Also, keep in mind that churches do not pay unemployment taxes for their employees, and ministers have special tax treatment, as well. Finally, pay particular attention to the formulation of the church budget, to ensure that it is conservatively managed to keep expenditures tightly in line with projected cash receipts.

Chapter 3
Tax Issues for Churches

Introduction

Because of their nonprofit status, churches need to be aware of several tax issues that apply to them – sometimes on a daily basis. In particular, the bookkeeper must keep track of donations and issue properly-worded acknowledgments to donors. These tracking and acknowledgment requirements are even more onerous when vehicles are being donated. There are also issues with pass-through donations that can be resolved by setting up a benevolence fund. We discuss these issues and more in the following sections.

Dealing with Donations

Churches routinely receive tax-deductible charitable contributions from the members of their congregations. The IRS imposes specific recordkeeping and substantiation rules[3] on both donors and churches, which we cover in this section.

Direct Donations

From the perspective of the church, the main requirement is to provide a written acknowledgment for any single contribution of $250 or more. The church does not incur a penalty if it does not do so, but without this acknowledgment, the donor cannot claim the tax deduction. Since the church certainly wants to continue receiving donations for an extended period of time, it needs to assist its donors by providing this acknowledgment. This should be a written statement that includes the following information:

- The name of the church
- The amount of the cash contribution
- A description of any non-cash contribution
- A statement that no goods or services were provided by the church in return for the contribution (if that was the case)
- A description and good faith estimate of the value of goods and services, if any, that the church provided in return for the contribution. This is needed so that the donor can reduce the amount of his or her contribution deduction by the fair market value of the goods and services provided. These goods and services may include cash, property, services, benefits or privileges, with the following exceptions:
    o Insubstantial goods or services, such as a coffee mug

---

[3] As stated in IRS Publication 1771, *Charitable Contributions – Substantiation and Disclosure Requirements*

- o Intangible religious benefits, such as admission to a religious cere-mony

> **Note:** Benefits that are not intangible religious benefits include education leading to a recognized degree, travel services and consumer goods.

- A statement that goods or services, if any, that the church provided in return for the contribution consisted entirely of intangible religious benefits, if that was the case

> **Note:** It is not necessary to include the donor's social security number or tax identification number on the acknowledgment document.

A separate acknowledgment can be provided for each single contribution of $250 or more, or one acknowledgment, such as an annual summary, to substantiate several individual contributions of $250 or more.

> **Note:** There is no IRS-approved acknowledgment form. A letter, postcard, or computer-generated form is acceptable, as long as it contains the preceding information.

A church can provide the acknowledgment electronically, such as via an email addressed to the donor.

Donation acknowledgments should be sent no later than January 31 of the year following a donation. For this acknowledgment to be considered contemporaneous with the contribution, a donor must receive it by the earlier of the date on which the return is filed or the due date (including extensions) of the return.

Unreimbursed Expenses

If a donor makes a single contribution of $250 or more in the form of unreimbursed expenses, such as paying for the food consumed during a church function, then he or she must obtain a written acknowledgment from the church that includes the following information:

- A description of the goods or services provided by the donor
- A statement of whether the church provided goods or services in return for the contribution
- A description and good faith estimate of the value of any goods or services that the church provided in return for the contribution
- A statement that goods or services, if any, that the church provided in return for the contribution consisted entirely of intangible religious benefits, if that was the case

Quid Pro Quo Contributions

A donor may make a payment that is partly a contribution and partly for goods and services provided by the church. This is known as a quid pro quo contribution. A church must provide a written disclosure statement to a donor when the amount paid by the donor in this situation is greater than $75. For example, a donor gives a church $100 in exchange for a concert ticket that has a fair market value of $40. In this case, the donor's tax deduction cannot exceed $60. Because the quid pro quo payment exceeds $75, the church must furnish a disclosure statement to the donor, even though the deductible amount does not exceed $75. A written disclosure statement for a quid pro quo contribution must include the following information:

- A statement that the amount of the contribution that is deductible for federal income tax purposes is limited to the excess of money contributed by the donor over the value of goods or services provided by the church
- A good-faith estimate of the fair market value of the goods or services

The IRS can charge a church a penalty of $10 when it does not provide a donor with a written disclosure related to a quid pro quo contribution of more than $75.

Written Acknowledgments

Here are several examples of acknowledgment phrases that could be sent to a church donor:

Thank you for your cash contribution of $___ that the First Baptist Church received on [date]. No goods or services were provided in exchange for your contribution.

Thank you for your cash contribution of $___ that the First Baptist Church received on [date]. In exchange for your contribution, we gave you an illustrated historical guide to the construction of the church, with an estimated fair market value of $50.

Thank you for your contribution of a used dining room table and matching chairs that the First Baptist Church received on [date]. No goods or services were provided in exchange for your contribution.

These acknowledgments should include the name and address of the church, which can be useful in case the IRS audits the records of a donor.

Vehicle Donations

A church may occasionally receive a donated vehicle. This is a proper activity for a nonprofit entity, as long as it does one of the following:

- It sells these donated vehicles and uses the proceeds exclusively to fund its charitable programs;
- It regularly uses the vehicles for a significant period of time to conduct activities that substantially further its charitable programs;

- It sells the vehicles after it makes a material improvement to them and then uses the proceeds to exclusively further its charitable programs; or
- It distributes the vehicles at a price significantly below fair market value to needy individuals in direct furtherance of its charitable purpose of relieving the poor and distressed or the underprivileged who are in need of a means of transportation.

A donor cannot deduct any single charitable contribution valued at $250 or more unless the church provides the donor with a contemporaneous written acknowledgment of the contribution. The information the church must provide in the acknowledgment depends on what it does with the vehicle and on its claimed value.[4]

There are several variations on what a church must report, depending on the value of the vehicle donated. We note the various disclosure requirements in the following paragraphs.

Vehicle Contributions of More Than $500

If a donor contributes a vehicle and claims its value to be more than $500, the church must provide a contemporaneous written acknowledgment to the donor that includes the following information:

- The donor's name and taxpayer identification number
- The vehicle identification number
- The date of the contribution and one of the following:
  - A statement that no goods or services were provided by the church in return for the donation, if that was the case;
  - A description and good faith estimate of the value of goods and services, if any, that the church provided in return for the donation; or
  - A statement that goods or services provided by the charity consisted entirely of intangible religious benefits, if that was the case.

If the church then sells the vehicle for more than $500, then in addition to the basic acknowledgments, it must also acknowledge the following:

- A statement that the vehicle was sold in an arm's length transaction between unrelated parties;
- The date when the vehicle was sold;
- The gross proceeds received from the sale; and
- A statement that the donor's deduction may not exceed the gross proceeds from the sale.

---

[4] As stated in IRS Publication 4302, *A Charity's Guide to Vehicle Donation*

There may be cases in which the church uses a donated vehicle to a significant extent. If so, then in addition to the basic acknowledgments, it must also acknowledge the following:

- State that the church intends to make a significant intervening use of the donated vehicle;
- A detailed statement of the intended use;
- A detailed statement of the duration of that use; and
- A certification that the vehicle will not be sold before completion of the use.

EXAMPLE

A member of the congregation of the First Baptist Church donates a small delivery van to the church, which is then used to deliver free lunches and dinners to the elderly during every day of the subsequent year. This use qualifies as a significant intervening use, because it is significant and substantially furthers the church's regularly conducted activity of delivering meals to those in need.

If the church plans to make a material improvement to a donated vehicle, then in addition to the basic acknowledgments, it must also acknowledge the following:

- A statement that the church intends to make a material improvement to the donated vehicle;
- A detailed description of the intended material improvement; and
- A certification that the vehicle will not be sold before completion of the improvement.

In all of the preceding cases, the church must provide the written acknowledgment to the donor within 30 days from the date of the vehicle's sale. This does not mean that the church must sell the vehicle in the year in which it receives it.

EXAMPLE

A vehicle is donated to the First Baptist Church on December 31, which is then sold by the church on January 15 of the following year. In this case, the acknowledgment is due by February 14.

If the church intends to make a significant intervening use of or material improvement to the vehicle, then the acknowledgment is due within 30 days from the date of the contribution.

One way to provide this acknowledgment is to use IRS Form 1098-C, *Contributions of Motor Vehicles, Boats, and Airplanes*, or a church may use its own form. However, the church must use the Form 1098-C to report the contribution to the IRS. A copy of the form appears in the following exhibit.

Sample Form 1098-C

7878	☐ VOID	☐ CORRECTED			
DONEE'S name, street address, city or town, state or province, country, ZIP or foreign postal code, and telephone no.		**1** Date of contribution	OMB No. 1545-1959	**Contributions of Motor Vehicles, Boats, and Airplanes**	
			Form **1098-C**		
		2a Odometer mileage	(Rev. November 2019)		
			For calendar year 20 ___		
		2b Year	**2c** Make	**2d** Model	
DONEE'S TIN	DONOR'S TIN	**3** Vehicle or other identification number			
DONOR'S name		**4a** ☐ Donee certifies that vehicle was sold in arm's length transaction to unrelated party			
Street address (including apt. no.)		**4b** Date of sale			
City or town, state or province, country, and ZIP or foreign postal code		**4c** Gross proceeds from sale (see instructions) $		**Copy A** For **Internal Revenue Service Center** File with Form 1096.	

5a ☐ Donee certifies that vehicle will not be transferred for money, other property, or services before completion of material improvements or significant intervening use

5b ☐ Donee certifies that vehicle is to be transferred to a needy individual for significantly below fair market value in furtherance of donee's charitable purpose

5c Donee certifies the following detailed description of material improvements or significant intervening use and duration of use

6a Did you provide goods or services in exchange for the vehicle? . . . . ▶ Yes ☐ No ☐

6b Value of goods and services provided in exchange for the vehicle $

6c Describe the goods and services, if any, that were provided. If this box is checked, donee certifies that the goods and services consisted solely of intangible religious benefits . . . . ▶ ☐

7 Under the law, the donor may not claim a deduction of more than $500 for this vehicle if this box is checked . . . . . ▶ ☐

For Privacy Act and Paperwork Reduction Act Notice, see the **current General Instructions for Certain Information Returns.**

Form **1098-C** (Rev. 11-2019)   Cat. No. 39732R   www.irs.gov/Form1098C   Department of the Treasury - Internal Revenue Service

For a written acknowledgment of a vehicle contribution deduction of more than $500, a penalty applies if a church knowingly furnishes the donor with a false or fraudulent acknowledgment, or knowingly fails to furnish an acknowledgment with the required information. In the case of an acknowledgment related to the sale of a vehicle, the penalty is either the gross proceeds from the sale or the product of the highest tax and the sales price stated on the acknowledgment, whichever amount is greater. In the case of an acknowledgment that is not based on gross proceeds, the penalty is either $5,000 or the product of the highest tax rate and the claimed value of the vehicle, whichever amount is greater.

EXAMPLE

The United Methodist Church receives a donated vehicle from a prominent member of its board, which it then sells. The gross proceeds from the sale are $300, but the church provides the donor with an acknowledgment stating that the gross proceeds were actually $1,000. The highest tax rate is currently 35%. The church is subject to a penalty for knowingly furnishing a false or fraudulent acknowledgment to the donor. The amount of the penalty is $350, which is the product of the $1,000 sale price stated in the acknowledgment and the maximum 35% tax rate, because this amount is greater than the $300 gross proceeds from the sale of the vehicle.

Vehicle Contributions of $500 or Less

If a donor is claiming a charitable contribution deduction of at least $250 but not more than $500 per vehicle, the acknowledgment must include the name of the church, a description of the vehicle, and one of the following:

- A statement that no goods or services were provided by the church in return for the donation, if that was the case;
- A description and good faith estimate of the value of goods or services, if any, that the church provided in return for the donation; or
- A statement that goods or services provided by the charity consisted entirely of intangible religious benefits, if that was the case.

For the written acknowledgment to be considered contemporaneous, a donor must receive the acknowledgment by the earlier of the date on which the donor files his individual federal income tax return for the year of the contribution, or the due date of the return. The church may use Form 1098-C as its acknowledgment to the donor, or use its own statement.

IRS Information Return for Donations

A church will need to file the Form 8282, *Donee Information Return*, with the IRS if it sells, exchanges, consumes, or otherwise disposes of donated property within three years after the date when it was originally received (this does not include donated vehicles). This filing is not needed if the appraisal value of the property at the time of the donation was $500 or less, or if the item was consumed or distributed in fulfilling the church's function as a tax-exempt organization. The form must be filed within 125 days of the date of property disposition.

Pass-Through Donations

There may be cases in which members of the congregation send money to a church, stipulating that it be forwarded to someone in need. For example, a member of the congregation is suffering with a medical problem, so the congregation wants to send money to her. In this case, the church is only acting as a pass-through organization, where it merely directs payments as intended by donors. When this is the case, the donations are treated as gifts to the designated individual, and so are not tax deductible for the donor. This means that such donations should not be included on the church's periodic summary of contributions that it sends to each donor. Another option is to include these items separately on the summary, noting that they are not tax-deductible.

In short, the church must have full control of any donated funds before they can be classified as tax deductible.

Note: If a church manages a donation campaign for a specific missionary, these donations *are* tax-deductible, because the church is both initiating and controlling the campaign, and the donations are being made to further the tax-exempt purpose of the church.

The Benevolence Fund

A good way to avoid the problem with pass-through donations is for a church to operate a *benevolence fund*, which is used by the church to support those in the local community who are in need. Because the church is deciding who receives funds, rather than donors, contributions to this fund are tax-deductible – as long as they are not designated by the donor to be for a specific recipient. To operate a benevolence fund, a church should have the following administrative details in place:

- *Define purpose.* State exactly what types of local needs the fund will provide assistance for, such as food and paying for utilities.
- *Define lack of resources.* Define the financial circumstances of the recipient that will trigger a payment from the fund, such as being unemployed or below a certain income level.
- *Approval process.* Define who must approve expenditures from the fund, such as a designated committee or the minister. This may also include a formal application for assistance, which is useful for proving that a standard process is being followed.
- *Check payments.* Where possible, make checks payable to the suppliers to whom the designated person owes money, rather than directly to him or her; doing so ensures that funds are not mis-spent.
- *Documentation.* Maintain records for what was spent and to whom it was given.

Note: Benevolence payments made to an employee of the church are taxable to the employee as wages, and so should also have payroll taxes withheld from them. The same rule applies to any expenses paid on behalf of an employee.

Donated Labor

Members of the church congregation routinely help out the organization by donating their time. For example, a tax practitioner could offer to complete the church's tax return for free, while a local CPA could offer to set up its accounting system for free. In all cases, the value of this donated labor is *not* tax-deductible for the donor.

Discounted Pricing on Purchases

A local business may offer substantial discounts on the goods or services it sells to a church. In all cases, the amount of this discount from the normal retail list price is *not* tax-deductible for the seller.

> **Tip:** It might be better for the local business to charge full-price for what it sells to the church and then make a donation in the amount of the discount that would otherwise have been given. The donation would be tax-deductible.

IRS-Mandated Records Retention

The Internal Revenue Service (IRS) requires that an employer retain all records of employment taxes for at least four years. These records should include the following:

- Employer identification number
- Amounts and dates of all wage, annuity, and pension payments
- The fair market value of in-kind wages paid
- The names, addresses, social security numbers, and occupations of employees
- Employee copies of Forms W-2 and W-2c that were returned to the church as undeliverable
- Date of employment for each employee
- Periods for which employees were paid while absent due to sickness or injury, and the amount and weekly rate of payments made to them
- Copies of employees' income tax withholding allowance certificates
- Dates and amounts of tax deposits made by the church and acknowledgment numbers for deposits made
- Copies of returns filed and the related confirmation numbers
- Records of fringe benefits and expense reimbursements provided to employees, including substantiation

Summary

The typical church, no matter how small it may be, will need to have rock-solid procedures for how it handles the tracking and acknowledgment of donations, since donors rely on this information when compiling their tax returns – and it pays to keep donors happy. The bookkeeper should devise an extensive procedure for how to deal with every type of donation, and check with the irs.gov website every year to ensure that the acknowledgment and reporting requirements stated there are accurately reflected in the church's donations procedure.

Chapter 4
Accounting Controls

Introduction

Churches tend to rely heavily on volunteers, who typically cannot spend an inordinate amount of time working on church accounting and finance issues. The same problem applies to ministers, who generally do not enter the profession with a strong skill set in business operations. Given these resource issues, the typical church has problems understanding and complying with accounting standards and taxation requirements, and will likely have problems running its accounting systems. These issues can result in the inadvertent waste of funds or outright fraud losses, and possibly tax-related penalties being imposed on the church. The solution to these issues is to have a strong set of accounting controls.

Accounting controls refer to the manner in which processes are configured to manage risk within an organization. The targets of accounting controls are as follows:

- To guard against the loss of church assets
- To ensure that church financial statements represent fairly its financial results, financial position, and cash flows
- To ensure that the church's objectives are met in an effective and efficient manner
- To ensure that all applicable laws and regulations are followed

In this chapter, we will cover the reasons why churches are especially in need of controls, and then delve into an array of controls that should be implemented.

The Nature of Controls

A system of accounting control is comprised of two types of controls, which are preventive controls and detective controls. *Preventive controls* are used to keep a loss or an error from occurring. Examples of preventive controls are segregated duties and the physical protection of assets. These controls are typically integrated into a process, so that they are applied on a continual basis. They are especially common when the severity of a loss is considered to be quite high, so that their imposition will lower the probability of any loss ever occurring.

Detective controls are designed to locate problems after they have occurred. Once problems have been detected, the board can take steps to mitigate the risk that they will occur again in the future, usually by altering the underlying process. An example of a detective control is a bank reconciliation, which can detect unexpected withdrawals from a bank account. Detective controls are considered to be less robust than a preventive control, since a preventive control keeps losses from ever occurring, while a detective control may result in initial losses before corrective changes can be implemented.

The Risk of Church Fraud

Those involved in the management of a church tend to have an education that is decidedly not in the area of business, which means that there is little knowledge of the controls needed to minimize the risk of fraud. Further, those involved in maintaining and overseeing the books are sometimes volunteers, and so have little time to conduct a thorough examination of controls or the details of the accounts. And even worse, those called upon to actually maintain the books are frequently among the more trusted people in the church, which means that their fraudulent activities tend to go on for quite a while before anyone decides to investigate. Here are several examples of actual fraud cases involving churches:

- *Bookkeeper theft.* A church bookkeeper wrote a series of checks to herself over several years, embezzling more than $50,000.
- *Bookstore theft.* A church bookstore employee sold himself merchandise after reducing retail prices on the store computer to a fraction of their normal price, and then resold these purchased books on the side to other church members for a "discounted" price.
- *Daycare theft.* The director of a church daycare operation stole $100,000 by intercepting cash paid by parents to pay tuition for their children. She then gave the church board a roster of attendees that did not include the students whose tuition she had stolen.
- *Gift cards.* A church member used the church credit card to buy herself a number of gift cards at local stores, which she then used on personal acquisitions. The purchases were never questioned, since the bookkeeper assumed that the purchases were made on behalf of the church.
- *Offering theft.* A church usher collected offerings in the sanctuary balcony and then pocketed loose bills on his way down the stairs. Over several years, he stole several thousand dollars.
- *Pastor theft.* A church board gave the pastor total control over the church's bank account and credit cards with no oversight, allowing him to spend $200,000 on clothing, vacations, meals, and other purchases. In another case, a pastor created one set of books to share with his board, and another set that incorporated the funds he had stolen from the church.

Church Controls

Given the inherent issues within a church, it makes sense to maintain a solid set of controls to minimize the occurrence of fraud. In addition, controls are needed to minimize the occurrence and severity of accounting errors, which will inevitably arise even when an experienced bookkeeper is maintaining the accounting records.

A solid system of controls starts at the top of the church organization, with its board. Ideally, the board should include at least one person who has a background in finance and accounting, and preferably more. In addition, the entire board should receive training in how to read the church's financial statements, how its system of controls works, and why they are used. In addition, the board should sponsor an annual business meeting for the church, to which all members are invited, in order to discuss all aspects of church operations, the state of its cash receipts, and how that cash is being used. Having a competent board has a trickle-down effect on the church, where everyone involved in the organization is more likely to abide by its policies and controls.

To make the board more effective in how it deals with accounting and finance issues, consider installing the following policies and controls:

- *Treasurer post.* Assign the treasurer role to a board member, preferably the one with the most finance and accounting experience. This person should not be the bookkeeper, since part of the treasurer's role is to monitor what the bookkeeper is doing.
- *Term limits.* Require all members of the board, and especially those serving in a financial capacity, to rotate off the board for a period of time, such as after three years have been served. This prevents anyone from acquiring an excessive degree of influence over the finances or purchasing decisions of the church.
- *Conflict of interest policy.* Issue a conflict of interest policy, so that the board members are aware of the extent to which they can personally do business with the church. This does not have to be an outright prohibition on business interactions, but it should clearly state what is and is not allowed.
- *Budget comparison.* Create an annual budget, which can then be compared to actual results to see if there are any unusual variances requiring further investigation. In essence, the budget creates expectations for financial results, which makes it an excellent monitoring tool.
- *Financials review.* Have the board examine the financial statements in detail every month, making it easier to spot and investigate irregularities.
- *Trend line analysis.* Have the board monitor cash receipts and expenditures on a trend line, by type, for an extended period of time. By doing so, unusual dips in receipts or spikes in expenditures will become more readily apparent, and can then be investigated in detail.
- *Periodic audit.* The board should hire an outside auditor to examine the church's books each year. The auditor should be able to render an opinion about whether the church's financial statements fairly present its actual financial results and financial position.
- *IRS notices.* All mailings from the Internal Revenue Service should be forwarded unopened to the board. By doing so, the bookkeeper will not be able to hide any theft of payroll tax remittances.

Below the level of the board, the next most critical control is the segregation of duties, which means that the person who has access to the accounting records should not also have access to church assets. For example, the person who has access to plate collections should not also be able to record plate collections information in the accounting system. Otherwise, the person could steal collected cash and then record a reduced amount of collections in the accounting records, thereby neatly eliminating all traces of the theft. As another example, the person who takes cash deposits to the bank should not also conduct the monthly bank reconciliation. Again, someone who steals from this deposit could alter the bank reconciliation to remove all traces of the theft.

EXAMPLE

A member of the congregation gives Sally Evans, the church bookkeeper, a $500 donation check. Ms. Evans deposits the check into a bank account that she controls and then sends the donor a receipt for the donation. The donor assumes that the church received the donation, while the board sees no mention of the donation in the church's accounting records.

A better arrangement, and one that shows the segregation of duties, is when members of the congregation are instructed to mail their donations to a bank lockbox address, where the envelopes are opened by bank employees and funds are deposited into the church's account. The bank then forwards the deposit information to the bookkeeper, who records the deposits in the church's accounting system.

In the latter case, the shifting of checks to a second party (the bank) eliminates the risk that the bookkeeper could steal funds and hide his or her tracks in the church's accounting records.

At a more detailed level, consider installing the controls described in the following sub-sections.

Offering Controls

In most churches, an offering plate is passed around the congregation, so that members can make contributions toward church operations. Since donations are largely in cash, the offering plate represents a golden opportunity for theft, especially when it is kept out of sight of the congregation for even a few moments. To prevent the loss of donated cash, consider implementing the following controls:

- *Fixed offering boxes.* Rather than passing an offering plate around the church, install a set of locked offering boxes that are affixed to the walls throughout the church. Doing so makes it much more difficult to steal offerings.
- *Sealed offerings.* Ask the congregation to put their offerings in sealed envelopes before putting them in the offering plate. Doing so makes it more difficult for someone else in the congregation to spot large offerings.
- *Sunday offering count.* Have more than one person count the Sunday offering. Doing so makes it more difficult for any one person to abscond with the funds. Better yet, rotate this job among a group of volunteers, so that no two people can conspire to jointly steal offerings. Further, do not let related parties (such as members of the same family) count the offering, since they are more likely to collude to steal cash. The results of the count should be stated on an offering sheet, for which a sample appeared earlier in this course.

- *For deposit only*. Endorse all checks to the church with the stamp "For Deposit Only," which keeps someone from diverting checks to their own bank account.
- *Deposit slip copy*. Fill out a deposit slip for cash to be sent to the bank, and keep a copy of it in the church safe. This copy should be compared to the deposit remittance form sent back by the bank, to ensure that the amount sent to the bank and received by it are the same. If the bank's record is lower than the amount on the church's copy of the deposit slip, it is possible that the person transporting the funds to the bank illicitly extracted some cash before making the deposit.
- *Immediate deposits*. Offerings are more likely to be in cash, and so may be stolen if left on the premises for long. Therefore, keep them locked in a safe for as long as they are on the premises, and deposit them at the bank as soon as possible.
- *Count and deposit reconciliation*. Always reconcile the initial offering counts to the amounts on the deposit slips provided by the bank, to see if any offerings were stolen prior to being deposited.
- *Statement issuance*. Send a periodic statement to all church members, listing the amounts and dates of their contributions to the church. This may elicit inquiries if members do not see their contributions on the report.

Mailed Check Receipt Controls

Some members of the congregation prefer to mail their donations to the church. If so, there is a risk that someone could intercept these mailings when they arrive at the church. A safer approach is to direct all mailed payments to a post office box, from which someone besides the bookkeeper extracts all mail. This designated pick-up person then brings the envelopes back to the church and opens them in the presence of another person, to ensure that no checks are stolen. These two people should jointly write down each check number, check amount, and payor name, and then sign this document, which is kept on file. Ideally, these checks should be immediately deposited at the bank, thereby leaving minimal opportunities for anyone to intercept them.

Donor Acknowledgment Controls

A good control over the handling of cash and checks is to send an acknowledgment letter to each donor. This should be done following the end of each year for tax purposes, but could be addressed more frequently, in order to give them a chance to spot irregularities. If a donor receives an acknowledgment for a smaller amount than was actually donated, then it is quite reasonable to expect that person to contact the church for an explanation. To encourage these donor contacts, include the contact information for a board member on the acknowledgment; the intent is to route all inquiries away from the bookkeeper, who is the most likely person to be engaged in fraudulent activity.

Another use for the donor acknowledgment letter is as a collection device. When donors have committed to ongoing pledge amounts (or perhaps a shorter-term set of donations for a special project), the letter can include the amount still to be paid, alongside the amount that has already been paid. This serves as a useful reminder regarding their future commitments to the church.

Fund Raising Controls

Churches may occasionally engage in fund raising activities for specific causes, such as building repairs or to support missionary activities. For example, a church might conduct a raffle, or charge fees to attend a charity event. In these situations, the following controls should be used:

- *Raffle – ticket numbering.* Preprint a unique identifying number on each raffle ticket, and track the range of these numbers handed out to each person. Then, when the cash from ticket sales is eventually returned along with any unsold tickets, verify that the cash forwarded to the church matches the number of tickets sold. When there is a cash shortfall, it may mean that the person responsible for them either pocketed the missing amount or lost track of the cash.
- *Raffle – cash tracking.* Once all cash has been received, reconcile it to the detail for what was received, and investigate any differences, noting them on a reconciliation spreadsheet. Then sign the spreadsheet to acknowledge responsibility for the count, and forward the cash to the bank to be deposited, along with a deposit slip.
- *Charity event.* When selling tickets at the door for a charity event, begin with a set of prenumbered tickets, noting the number of the first and last tickets sold. Then compare the total amount of cash received to the numeric range of the tickets sold, to see if every ticket has been accounted for. For example, if the range of ticket numbers is from 1000 to 1320, then 320 tickets have been sold, and at a price of $10 per ticket, this means that there should be $3,200 of cash receipts. If the cash receipts are actually lower, then it is possible that some of the cash payments were intercepted.

Personnel Controls

The compensation cost for church personnel is likely to be the most significant expense for any church, even if the only person being paid is the minister. Given its size, personnel costs need especially detailed controls. Consider whether the following controls should be used:

- *Qualifications review.* It is quite common for paid church positions to be filled by members of the congregation, or their friends or family. This is fine, as long as the persons hired are qualified for their positions. Consequently, the board should conduct a review of applicant resumes before hires are made, to ensure that the persons hired are reasonably qualified.
- *Background checks.* Run background checks and annual credit reports on anyone directly involved with the church's finances, to see if there is any evidence of financial trouble or prior convictions.

- *Fidelity bond.* Acquire a fidelity bond, which reimburses the church for losses caused by employee actions, such as embezzlement or theft. This bond may cover all employees, or it may only be targeted at losses caused by specific employees. The insurer will require the church to engage in certain employment screening activities, to reduce the risk of hiring someone who is more likely to steal from the church.
- *Vacation requirement.* Require the church bookkeeper to take all awarded vacation time, every year. This is done to keep the person from maintaining any ongoing frauds on a year-round basis, thereby presenting opportunities to spot them in his or her absence.
- *Timesheet approvals.* All timesheets should be submitted to the supervisor of an employee, who signs off on and then forwards them to the bookkeeper, who loads them into the payroll system for processing. The result is a preliminary payroll register, which the church treasurer should review and approve before the payroll is finalized and payments are issued.
- *Outsourced payroll.* Shift the payroll processing function to a third party. Doing so ensures that payroll tax remittances will be forwarded to the government. When payroll processing is kept in-house, there is a possibility that the bookkeeper could pocket these remittances and keep the board from learning about them.

Procurement Controls

A church may need to engage the services of suppliers for substantial amounts of money. When this is the case, consider installing the following controls:

- *Contract examination.* Whenever there is a material, ongoing arrangement by the church to make purchases, the board should conduct a periodic examination of these contracts. The intent is to locate situations in which prices are clearly too high, and to also spot cases in which contracts were given to parties related to the congregation. The latter situation is not necessarily bad, but introduces the risk of overbilling.
- *Contract re-bidding.* The board should require a re-bid of the church's more material contracts on an annual basis, and solicit several bidders. Doing so ensures that the church is obtaining a reasonable market-based price for each contract.
- *Budget authorization.* Automatically allow purchasing within the mandates of the annual church budget, but require board approval for material expenditures outside of what was authorized in the budget.

Payables Controls

The processing of accounts payable should always be a highly regimented process, rich in controls, since a flaw anywhere in this process presents an opportunity for fraud. Consider installing the following controls to minimize losses:

- *Invoice documentation requirement.* Mandate that all payments made by the church be supported by an invoice from the applicable supplier. Or, if a church member is requesting reimbursement, only do so if the person can show a valid receipt for the purchase.
- *Invoice approval requirement.* Mandate that all invoices exceeding a materiality threshold (such as $250) be approved before they are entered into the accounting system. Doing so ensures that unapproved invoices are not inadvertently paid. To be even more conservative, have the board approve the larger invoices (such as anything exceeding $5,000).
- *Check storage.* Ensure that blank check stock is locked up when not in use, to minimize the risk that someone could steal checks and fill them out for personal gain.
- *Check signer restriction.* The bookkeeper should not be an authorized check signer. Otherwise, it would be all too easy for the bookkeeper to issue a check to himself (or a fake supplier that he controls), sign the check, and cash it. There tend not to be many options for check signers among the congregation; typically, this responsibility falls on a member of the board.
- *Avoidance of signature stamps.* Forbid the use of a signature stamp, since anyone gaining access to it could illicitly authorize any number of check payments.
- *Two signatures requirement.* Mandate that two people sign each check over a certain amount, to ensure that multiple people are reviewing the larger expenditures. However, keep in mind that most banks will not withhold payment on a check that does not have the required number of signatures on it, so this is a relatively ineffective control.

> **Tip:** Do not authorize too many check signers, since a nefarious bookkeeper could submit separate copies of the same invoice to multiple check signers, and retain the additional payments for his personal use.

- *ACH debits.* An ACH debit is an automatic electronic withdrawal of funds from a church's bank account in order to pay a bill. This approach is most commonly applied by larger suppliers that bill on a recurring basis, such as the power company. It is easy for these payments to fall outside of the normal invoice approval process, since they do not involve check payments. To mitigate this concern, present all ACH debits to the board on a monthly basis, so that they are aware of the amounts being paid.
- *Marking of paid invoices.* Once they have been paid, mark all invoices as paid, or perforate them with the word "paid." Doing so reduces the possibility that invoices will be paid twice, though the accounting software should flag any invoice numbers that have already been paid.
- *Storage of paid invoices.* Staple the supporting supplier invoice documentation to a copy of each check paid, and file this documentation by supplier name. In situations where a supplier is paid quite rarely, file the

documentation in a "Miscellaneous" folder for a letter range. For example, an invoice from Holmes Candlemakers (paid once yearly) could be filed in a folder labeled "Miscellaneous G-I," which contains all miscellaneous invoices from suppliers whose names begin with the letters "G" through "I". This approach is useful for minimizing the loss of backup documentation.

- *Check register review.* The check register is a listing of all checks issued by a church during a specific period of time. The register states the payment dates, check numbers, payment amounts, and payee names for all check payments. Someone other than the bookkeeper should review this report to see if there are any duplicate payments or other payments that appear to be suspicious in any way.

Credit Card Controls

A church may have its own credit card, or congregation members may make purchases on behalf of the church using their own credit cards, and then forward the receipts to the bookkeeper for reimbursement. In either case, all purchases must be approved by someone other than the person who made the purchase, such as a member of the board. Additional controls should be placed on the use of a church credit card, such as keeping it locked in a secure place, tightly controlling who is allowed to use it, and capping the amount that may be charged to it on a daily basis (thereby capping the total amount of any illicit charges that may be made).

A final control over the use of credit cards is to require card users to fill out a form at the end of each month, on which they state each line item from the credit card statement, the nature of the expense, and its purpose. The bookkeeper uses this information to charge expenditures to the correct asset or expense account in the accounting system.

Petty Cash Controls

Petty cash is a small amount of cash that is kept on the premises in order to make incidental cash payments and reimbursements, such as for delivered meals. Since it can take time to prepare a check payment, petty cash may be the best alternative in a time-sensitive situation. The petty cash box is typically funded with a small amount of cash, such as $250. When someone needs to be reimbursed from petty cash, a payment slip is filled out and signed by both the recipient and the petty cash custodian, which means that the cash balance in the account has been reduced and replaced by evidence of payment. Consequently, the payment slips and remaining cash in the box should always match the original petty cash funding amount. For example, if petty cash is funded with an initial $250 and $110 are later spent for meals delivered to the church, then the petty cash box should now contain $140 of cash and $110 of payment slips (to which are attached the supplier's meal invoices).

There are several control points to consider for petty cash. One is to lock up the petty cash box when it is not in use, since someone could steal the entire box. Another control is to give the petty cash custodian proper training in how to use it, along with a printed procedure that is kept in the box. And most importantly, someone other than the petty cash custodian should audit the petty cash box at unannounced intervals, to see if the combination of cash and payment slips still equals the original petty cash funding amount. When this amount is too low, someone has likely stolen cash from the petty cash box.

Fixed Asset Controls

The largest assets in a church are not exactly subject to theft, such as the building, the church van, and its organ. However, this still leaves many smaller items of relatively high value that can be stolen, such as electronics and media equipment. This is a particular concern in the church environment, where there may not be staff on the premises at all times, and when many people routinely cycle through the public areas. To minimize fixed asset losses, ensure that vulnerable assets are kept in locked rooms. Also, assign responsibility for these assets, so that someone knows where they are at all times. Further, keep detailed records of these items, including their descriptions, purchase dates, and purchase amounts; this information may be needed when filing claims with the church's insurer for the replacement of stolen assets. It can also be useful to affix a unique tag number to each asset and use this information to conduct a periodic fixed asset audit, to ensure that all items are still present and accounted for.

Additional Control Topics

A particular concern is the involvement of the minister in any financial matters. This should be minimized, for two reasons. First, any minister has a vast number of responsibilities, and so cannot devote sufficient time to financial issues. And more importantly, the minister needs to be above reproach when it comes to any monetary issues. To do so, this person should never take any cash or check offerings from members of the congregation, and should have no check signing authority. However, this does not mean that the minister should be ignorant of the church's finances; on the contrary, he or she should have a good understanding of the church's financial statements, in order to fully appreciate the financial viability of the church.

Low-Cost Church Controls

Churches generally operate with little excess cash, so some of the preceding control recommendations might seem to be beyond their financial resources. When this is the case, there are some lower-cost alternatives available. They may not be as effective as our primary recommendations, but can still improve the control environment. Here are some low-cost control suggestions:

- *Periodic audit.* Audit firms are quite expensive, so paying one to conduct a full audit each year might appear to be a profligate use of cash. If so, consider hiring an auditor to conduct a review, rather than an audit. An auditor who conducts a review must perform *analytical procedures* and make inquiries of the church concerning its financial statements. Based on these investigations, the auditor can provide limited assurance that the financial statements do not need any material modifications. If the church cannot even afford a review, then form an audit committee from church members and have them review the books.

- *Segregation of duties.* The segregation of duties concept can be an exceedingly difficult one to implement in a small church, where it may be difficult to find enough people willing to participate in accounting activities. If so, a reasonable workaround is for the minister to either be in charge of the handling of cash or its recordation, but not both. A volunteer can then be called upon to fulfill the other function; a further control is to rotate out this volunteer at regular intervals, so that any fraudulent activities could only be conducted for a short period of time. In this situation, it also makes sense to only authorize someone from the board to sign checks.

Summary

In this chapter, we described a large number of controls that could be installed in a church. It might seem unnecessary that a church, which is generally a relatively small organization, would need to install so many controls. However, because church financial functions tend to be concentrated with one person or just a few volunteers, it is relatively common for theft to occur in this environment. And, given the skimpy finances of most churches, even a modest theft could imperil the viability of the organization. Consequently, we recommend that *all* of the controls recommended in this chapter be installed.

Glossary

A

Accounting controls. The manner in which processes are configured to manage risk within an organization.

Accrual. A journal entry that allows a business to record expenses and revenues for which it expects to expend cash or receive cash, respectively, in a future period.

Accrual basis. When revenue is recorded when earned and expenses are recorded when consumed.

Analytical procedures. Comparisons of different sets of financial and operational information, to see if historical relationships are continuing forward into the period under review.

Asset. An item of economic value that is expected to yield a benefit in future periods.

B

Base unit. The definition of what constitutes a fixed asset.

Benevolence fund. A fund that is used to help people in a church or its surrounding community.

C

Capitalization limit. A threshold above which expenditures for assets with long lives are capitalized.

Cash basis. When revenue is recorded when cash is received from customers, and expenses are recorded when cash is paid to suppliers and employees.

Chart of accounts. A list that states every account in the general ledger.

Credit. An accounting entry that either increases a liability or equity account, or decreases an asset or expense account.

D

Debit. An accounting entry that either increases an asset or expense account, or decreases a liability or equity account.

Depreciation. The planned, gradual reduction in the recorded value of an asset over its useful life by charging it to expense.

Detective controls. Controls that locate problems after they have occurred.

Double entry accounting. A record keeping system under which every transaction is recorded in at least two accounts.

F

Fixed asset. Property that is intended to be used for an extended period of time, and which exceeds an organization's capitalization limit.

Fund. A designated amount of resources that has been set aside for a specific purpose.

Fund accounting. A system for tracking the amount of cash assigned to different purposes and the usage of that cash.

G

General ledger. The master set of accounts that summarize all transactions occurring within an organization.

J

Journal entry. A formalized method for recording an accounting transaction in a double entry accounting system.

M

Minister. A member of the clergy, especially in Protestant churches.

N

Net assets. The total assets of a church, minus its total liabilities.

P

Payroll cycle. The length of time between two payrolls.

Petty cash. A small amount of cash that is kept on the premises in order to make incidental cash payments and reimbursements, such as for delivered meals.

Preventive controls. Controls that are used to keep a loss or an error from occurring.

Q

Quid pro quo contribution. A payment made to a nonprofit entity by a donor, partly as a contribution and partly for goods or services provided to the donor by the nonprofit.

S

Step cost. A cost that tends to increase sharply at discrete points, rather than gradually as activity volume rises.

Index

www.ingramcontent.com/pod-product-compliance
Lightning Source LLC
Chambersburg PA
CBHW051417200326
41520CB00023B/7267